CHARLES F. STANLEY

LIFE PRINCIPLES

BIBLE

SECOND EDITION

BY THE BOOK SERIES:
REVELATION

CHARLES F. STANLEY
GENERAL EDITOR

THOMAS NELSON
Since 1798

www.ThomasNelson.com

The Charles F. Stanley Life Principles Bible, 2nd Edition, Revelation
Copyright © 2009, 2019 by Charles F. Stanley
Published in Nashville, Tennessee, by Thomas Nelson.
Thomas Nelson is a registered trademark of HarperCollins Christian Publishing, Inc.

Holy Bible, New King James Version, copyright © 1982 by Thomas Nelson.

Library of Congress Control Number: 2021931462

This Bible was set in the Thomas Nelson NKJV Comfort Print Typeface, created at the 2K/DENMARK type foundry.

Printed in the United States of America

21 22 23 24 25 26 27 [TRM] 12 11 10 9 8 7 6 5 4 3 2 1

BY THE BOOK SERIES

You are holding a single book of the Bible from the *Charles F. Stanley Life Principles Bible*. Even though it is only one book, it certainly does not lack content. This robust edition, which includes interleaved journal pages, offers a compact and portable way to study this special last book of the Bible. It also gives you a taste of what the full *Life Principles Bible* has to offer. If you find your study of Revelation as rewarding as we expect you will, consider obtaining a copy of the full Bible to continue your studies.

Keep in mind that this book is taken in its entirety from the *Life Principles Bible* with no major revisions or deletions. Therefore, it may contain cross references and study notes that point to other parts of the Bible. In addition, some notes may build from previous notes and/or point to other notes outside of the Book of Revelation. Again, this is simply a taste.

> *Oh, taste and see that the LORD is good;*
> *blessed is the man who trusts in Him!*
>
> Psalm 34:8

Welcome to
The Charles F. Stanley
Life Principles Bible®

Dear Friend,

When I was a young man, I had the opportunity to spend two very important and intensely rich weeks with my grandfather. He was a godly man, who loved the Lord with his whole heart. And though he did not have a formal education, he was tremendously wise and had great insight into the principles of God's Word. One of the first things he taught me was this: "Obey God and leave the consequences to Him. No matter what He tells you to do, do it and trust Him for the outcome." This is a principle that I have learned to live by each day. There is nothing too great for God. He is above and over all things. He is sovereign, omnipotent, and omnipresent. My greatest needs are all met within Him.

The second thing he told me was to read my Bible every day. After his death, I was given his Bible and knew the moment it was placed in my hands that he had lived what he preached. Every page was well worn, and most bore the marks of intense Bible study. Over the years, I have come to realize that God's Word offers the wisdom and insight I need at every turn. I cannot and never will encounter anything that is beyond Him and the principles He has written in Scripture.

The Christian life is a wondrous adventure, full of twists and turns, good times and also difficult challenges. Through all of it, God's Word is our greatest resource for insight, wisdom, hope, and guidance. Every problem we face has its solution in the Word of God. Where there is a need for comfort, peace, or courage, He provides it. To find His wisdom, there is simply no substitute for spending time alone with Him in prayer and the study of His Scriptures. Each year I receive countless letters from people who ask if there is a way for them to know God's will for their lives. The answer is yes. But before He will reveal this to us, we need to get to know Him— the way He thinks, acts, and demonstrates His love for us.

The Charles F. Stanley Life Principles Bible was written to provide powerful insight into the principles written in God's Word. These lessons are ones that I have learned personally during my fifty years of ministry, and it is my prayer that they will become principles that God will use in your life to teach you more about Himself and to draw you closer to His heart. There is no substitute for a personal relationship with Jesus Christ. This is the very core of God's message to each one of us. If we want to know Him, we need to get to know His Son.

The various features and helps included in this Bible are not designed to be a substitute for personal Bible study. Instead, they are meant to be signposts to help you journey even deeper into God's Word. You can pray and ask Him to open your heart to His Word so that you will understand His principles and learn to apply them to your life. They are timeless.

In this resource, I have highlighted many of the most crucial ones so that you might grow in your faith and learn to trust God in every area of your life. By surrendering our lives to Him and then asking Him to teach us His truths, we can put into practice the life principles He has given us. We also can learn to live a life of spiritual success and avoid the snares and traps that would lead to ineffectiveness, heartache, and disappointment. God's greatest goals for your life are for you to know Him and then for you to live your life committed to Him.

Throughout this Bible you'll find several features designed to help you get the most out of your time in God's Word:

- **Book introductions** to each of the 66 books of the Bible offer helpful background information and alert you to some of the most crucial Life Principles found in each book.
- **Life Principles** articles highlight thirty of the Bible's most critical principles for

successful Christian living. They focus on crucial topics such as building intimacy with God, prayer, obedience, dealing with adversity, and more.

- **What the Bible Says About** articles bring scriptural insight to bear on a wide variety of topics of special concern to all believers in Christ: the Holy Spirit's guidance, the process of spiritual growth, experiencing forgiveness, listening to God, and many more.
- **Answers to Life's Questions** focus on the many challenges we face in our Christian faith as we try to live for God in a world often hostile to our growth in grace. How do we deal with jealousy or bitterness, or how do we gain God's mind in a tough situation? You'll find those kinds of questions answered here.
- **Life Examples** briefly consider the lives of scores of God's choice servants spotlighted in the Bible, with a special eye toward discerning how their experiences can encourage and help us.
- **Life Lessons** offer more than 2,500 insights into individual Bible verses and passages, emphasizing the practical and personal nature of God's Word to us.
- **God's Promises** highlight more than 300 of the Lord's promises to His people—promises meant to encourage, strengthen, and fill us with hope.
- The **Life Principles Indexes** and the **Promises Index**, located in the front of the Bible, give you a convenient way to study God's principles and promises throughout the Old and New Testaments.

As you read God's Holy Word, I encourage you to keep a notebook and a pen nearby so you can record the date and time of your interaction with the Lord. As He shows you fresh truths, write them down. If He convicts you of a certain sin or attitude, make a note of it and write your prayer confessing that particular sin. If He gives you a moment of joy, praise Him in writing. If you have questions, write those down as well, and ask the Holy Spirit to teach you God's truth for every situation. You will also want to use other Bible helps, such as dictionaries and commentaries, to shed light on difficult passages. Don't try to read large portions of the Bible at one time;

sit and meditate on one verse or one portion of a verse. Also, be sure to ask the Holy Spirit to help you understand what that verse means and how to make a practical application of it.

If you find a promise, a provision, a requirement, or a commandment that you sense He is giving you, record it in your notebook. Doing this faithfully day after day helps you to begin to think the way God thinks. You will start to use "the mind of Christ," which the Bible says you have (1 Cor. 2:16). You also will begin to see life from His perspective, which will help you understand how you need to live each day. The more you learn about God, the richer your life will become through the knowledge of His Word.

By surrendering your life to Him and following His principles of obedience, you will be on the road to great blessing and reward. You will have the ability to live a liberated life—free from sin and full of God's goodness, grace, and mercy. When you obey Him, you can anticipate that He will reveal exciting new things to you. Never forget that the key to crossing any bridge successfully is faith and obedience. Jesus said, "He who has My commandments and keeps them, it is he who loves Me. And he who loves Me will be loved by My Father, and I will love him and manifest Myself to him" (John 14:21). The act of understanding His Word and obeying Him comes from personal growth and intimacy with the Lord. The closer you draw to Him, the more you will know about Him.

This is what makes the journey into His truth so exciting. You have the guarantee that the Lord will reveal more of Himself and His goodness to you as you mature in your relationship with Him. He also will pour out His blessings on your life until it overflows with joy, peace, and goodness; and I believe that as you put into practice His principles, you will enjoy the abundant life that Jesus so earnestly desires to give to you (John 10:10). It is my prayer that you will not only discover the treasure of His infinite love and truth, but that you will walk in the light of His goodness each and every day. There is only one way to do this, and it is by knowing God through prayer and the study of His Word.

Charles F. Stanley

PREFACE TO THE
NEW KING JAMES VERSION®

To understand the heart behind the New King James Version, one need look no further than the stated intentions of the original King James scholars: "Not to make a new translation . . . but to make a good one better." The New King James Version is a continuation of the labors of the King James translators, unlocking for today's readers the spiritual treasures found especially in the Authorized Version of the Holy Bible.

While seeking to maintain the excellent *form* of the traditional English Bible, special care has also been taken to preserve the work of *precision* which is the legacy of the King James translators.

Where new translation has been necessary, the most complete representation of the original has been rendered by considering the definition and usage of the Hebrew, Aramaic, and Greek words in their contexts. This translation principle, known as complete equivalence, seeks to preserve accurately all of the information in the text while presenting it in good literary form.

In addition to accuracy, the translators have also sought to maintain those lyrical and devotional qualities that are so highly regarded in the King James Version. The thought flow and selection of phrases from the King James Version have been preserved wherever possible without sacrificing clarity.

The format of the New King James Version is designed to enhance the vividness, devotional quality, and usefulness of the Bible. Words or phrases in italics indicate expressions in the original language that require clarification by additional English words, as was done in the King James Version. Poetry is structured as verse to reflect the form and beauty of the passage in the original language. The covenant name of God was usually translated from the Hebrew as LORD or GOD, using capital letters as shown, as in the King James Version. This convention is also maintained in the New King James Version when the Old Testament is quoted in the New.

The Hebrew text used for the Old Testament is the 1967/1977 Stuttgart edition of the *Biblia Hebraica*, with frequent comparisons to the Bomberg edition of 1524–25. Ancient versions and the Dead Sea Scrolls were consulted, but the Hebrew is followed wherever possible. Significant variations, explanations, and alternate renderings are mentioned in footnotes.

The Greek text used for the New Testament is the one that was followed by the King James translators: the traditional text of the Greek-speaking churches, called the Received Text or Textus Receptus, first published in 1516. Footnotes indicate significant variants from the Textus Receptus as found in two other editions of the Greek New Testament:

(1) NU-Text: These variations generally represent the Alexandrian or Egyptian text type as found in the critical text published in the twenty-seventh edition of the Nestle-Aland Greek New Testament (N) and in the United Bible Societies' third edition (U).

(2) M-Text: These variations represent readings found in the text of *The Greek New Testament According to the Majority Text*, which follows the consensus of the majority of surviving New Testament manuscripts.

The textual notes in the New King James Version make no evaluation, but objectively present the facts about variant readings.

THE
REVELATION
OF JESUS CHRIST

• • •

Just as Genesis is the book of beginnings, so Revelation is the book of completion. In it, we see how God finalizes the divine program of redemption and vindicates His holy name before all creation.

Although the Gospels and Epistles contain numerous prophecies, only Revelation focuses primarily on prophetic events. It borrows heavily from Old Testament symbols and passages and seems to have a special connection to the Book of Daniel. Because of this potent imagery, it is often difficult to know in Revelation when the author is speaking literally and when he is speaking symbolically.

Revelation also features several high moments of worship in which the residents of heaven and the saints of God praise the Lord for His holy character and righteous judgments. These extraordinary times of worship are usually presented as joyful songs of praise (Rev. 4:8–11; 5:8–14; 7:9–12; 11:15–18; 15:2–4; 16:5–7; 19:1–7).

The title of this book in the Greek text is *Apokalypsis Ioannou*, "Revelation of John." It is also known as the Apocalypse, a transliteration of the word *apokalypsis*, meaning "unveiling, disclosure, or revelation." Thus, the book unveils what otherwise could not be known. A better title comes from the first verse, the "Revelation of Jesus Christ." This could be taken as a revelation that came from Christ or as a revelation about Christ. Both are appropriate.

Revelation was originally written to seven local churches in Asia Minor (modern Turkey), but its message applies to all Christians everywhere. Jesus is coming again in great power and glory, and His certain return should motivate us every day to Spirit-filled, loving action on His behalf.

THEMES: Revelation centers around awesome visions and extraordinary symbols of the resurrected Christ who alone has authority to judge the earth, to remake it, and to rule it in righteousness.

AUTHOR: The apostle John wrote Revelation during his exile on the island of Patmos.

TIME: Most scholars believe the book was written circa A.D. 95.

STRUCTURE: Revelation starts out with a vision of Jesus Christ (ch. 1), followed by a message from Him to the seven churches in Asia Minor (chs. 2–3), followed by another vision of Jesus (chs. 4–5). The remainder of the book (chs. 6–22) employs difficult symbolism and startling imagery to picture the final triumph of good over evil.

AS YOU READ REVELATION, WATCH FOR THE LIFE PRINCIPLES THAT PLAY AN IMPORTANT ROLE IN THIS BOOK:

19. Anything you hold too tightly, you will lose. See *Revelation 3:16; 9:6.*

16. Whatever you acquire outside of God's will eventually turns to ashes. See *Revelation 6:17.*

10. If necessary, God will move heaven and earth to show us His will. See *Revelation 10:7.*

30. An eager anticipation of the Lord's return keeps us living productively. See *Revelation 22:12.*

Introduction and Benediction

1 The Revelation of Jesus Christ, *a*which God gave Him to show His servants— things which must ¹shortly take place. And *b*He sent and signified *it* by His angel to His servant John, *2a*who bore witness to the word of God, and to the testimony of Jesus Christ, to all things *b*that he saw. *3a*Blessed *is* he who reads and those who hear the words of this prophecy, and keep those things which are written in it; for *b*the time *is* near.

Greeting the Seven Churches

⁴John, to the seven churches which are in Asia:

Grace to you and peace from Him *a*who is and *b*who was and who is to come, *c*and from the seven Spirits who are before His throne, ⁵and from Jesus Christ, *a*the faithful *b*witness, the *c*first-born from the dead, and *d*the ruler over the kings of the earth.

To Him *e*who ¹loved us *f*and washed us from our sins in His own blood, ⁶and has *a*made us ¹kings and priests to His God and Father, *b*to Him *be* glory and dominion forever and ever. Amen.

⁷Behold, He is coming with *a*clouds, and every eye will see Him, even *b*they who pierced Him. And all the tribes of the earth will mourn because of Him. Even so, Amen.

8a"I am the Alpha and the Omega, ¹*the* Beginning and *the* End," says the ²Lord, *b*"who is and who was and who is to come, the *c*Almighty."

Vision of the Son of Man

⁹I, John, ¹both your brother and *a*companion in the tribulation and *b*kingdom

1:1 *a* John 3:32 *b* Rev. 22:6 ¹*quickly* or *swiftly* 1:2 *a*1 Cor. 1:6 *b*1 John 1:1 1:3 *a* Luke 11:28 *b* James 5:8 1:4 *a* Ex. 3:14 *b* John 1:1
c [Is. 11:2] 1:5 *a* John 8:14 *b* Is. 55:4 *c* [Col. 1:18] *d* Rev. 17:14 *e* John 13:34 *f* Heb. 9:14 ¹NU *loves us and freed*; M *loves us and washed* 1:6 *a*1 Pet. 2:5, 9 *b*1 Tim. 6:16 ¹NU, M *a kingdom* 1:7 *a* Matt. 24:30 *b* Zech. 12:10–14 1:8 *a* Is. 41:4 *b* Rev. 4:8; 11:17
c Is. 9:6 ¹NU, M *omit the Beginning and the End* ²NU, M *Lord God* 1:9 *a* Phil. 1:7 *b* [2 Tim. 2:12] ¹NU, M *omit both*

⊢ LIFE LESSONS ⊢

■ 1:3 — Many ignore the Book of Revelation because they believe it is too difficult to understand. Yet there is a blessing for those who both read and keep it — making whatever adjustments are necessary to obey what God requires of us in His Word. Why is Revelation a special blessing? Because there is no other book that so exalts the Lord Jesus Christ.

■ 1:4 — *Grace* was a typical Greek greeting of the first century, while *peace* served as the typical Hebrew greeting. This book is for everyone, both Jew and Gentile alike. Also, John explains that this is a special message for believers from the triune Godhead. "Who is and who was and who is to come" is God the Father, the "I AM" (Ex. 3:14). The seven spirits are a symbol of the Holy Spirit (Is. 11:1, 2). And of course, it is also "from Jesus Christ . . . who loved us and washed us from our sins in His own blood" (Rev. 1:5).

■ 1:5 — Several individuals in the Bible (before Jesus) had been raised from the dead. But all of them — the Shunammite's son (2 Kin. 4:35), Jairus's daughter (Mark 5:42), and Lazarus (John 11:44) — all died a second time. Yet Jesus conquered death for all eternity, and everyone who believes in Him will live forever.

■ 1:6 — In A.D. 70, the Romans destroyed the city of Jerusalem and the temple, enslaving and persecuting the Jews. Many believers wondered what had happened — had the Lord Jesus failed them? The promise that God had given of fully restoring them as a nation in the Promised Land seemed so far away (Ezek. 36:24–30). John wrote to remind them that although the Lord would keep His specific promises to Israel, His true kingdom was not of this world (John 18:36). He would come again in glory to redeem His own forever, regardless of the situation on earth.

■ 1:7 — The Second Coming of Christ will follow the seven-year Tribulation period, which is marked by judgment upon the earth (Zech. 12:10). During the Tribulation, the Lord will pour out His wrath on those who reject Him, and although many will be destroyed, multitudes of people will be saved. Then the whole earth will witness His return as the King of kings. He will finish cleansing the earth of ungodliness and set up His millennial reign.

■ 1:9 — Located in the Aegean Sea, off the coast of Asia south of Ephesus, Patmos was used by the Romans as a penal colony. John was banished there by Emperor Domitian circa A.D. 95, when he was close to ninety years of age. God used this imprisonment as an opportunity to give him an astounding look into the future, as well as to the coming heavenly kingdom.

and patience of Jesus Christ, was on the island that is called Patmos for the word of God and for the testimony of Jesus Christ. [10a]I was in the Spirit on [b]the Lord's Day, and I heard behind me [c]a loud voice, as of a trumpet, [11]saying, [1]"I am the Alpha and the Omega, the First and the Last," and, "What you see, write in a book and send *it* to the seven churches [2]which are in Asia: to Ephesus, to Smyrna, to Pergamos, to Thyatira, to Sardis, to Philadelphia, and to Laodicea."

[12]Then I turned to see the voice that spoke with me. And having turned [a]I saw seven golden lampstands, [13a]and in the midst of the seven lampstands [b]*One* like the Son of Man, [c]clothed with a garment down to the feet and [d]girded about the chest with a golden band. [14]His head and [a]hair *were* white like wool, as white as snow, and [b]His eyes like a flame of fire; [15a]His feet *were* like fine brass, as if refined in a furnace, and [b]His voice as the sound of many waters; [16a]He had in His right hand seven stars, [b]out of His mouth went a sharp two-edged sword, [c]and His countenance *was* like the sun shining in its strength. [17]And [a]when I saw Him, I fell at His feet as dead. But [b]He laid His right hand on me, saying [1]to me, "Do not be afraid; [c]I am the First and the Last. [18a]I *am* He who lives, and was dead, and behold, [b]I am alive forevermore. Amen. And [c]I have the keys of [1]Hades and of Death. [19]Write the things which you have [a]seen, [b]and the things which are, [c]and the things which will take place after this. [20]The [1]mystery of the seven stars which you saw in My right hand, and the seven golden lampstands: The seven stars are [a]the [2]angels of the seven churches, and [b]the seven lampstands [3]which you saw are the seven churches.

The Loveless Church

2 "To the [1]angel of the church of Ephesus write,

['These] things says [a]He who holds the seven stars in His right hand, [b]who walks in the midst of the seven golden lampstands: [2a]"I know your works, your labor, your [1]patience, and that you cannot [2]bear those who are evil. And [b]you have tested those [c]who say they are apostles and are not, and have found them liars; [3]and you

1:10 [a] Acts 10:10 [b] Acts 20:7 [c] Rev. 4:1 1:11 [1] NU, M omit *"I am the Alpha and the Omega, the First and the Last," and,* [2] NU, M omit *which are in Asia* 1:12 [a] Ex. 25:37 1:13 [a] Rev. 2:1 [b] Ezek. 1:26 [c] Dan. 10:5 [d] Rev. 15:6 1:14 [a] Dan. 7:9 [b] Dan. 10:6 1:15 [a] Ezek. 1:7 [b] Ezek. 1:24; 43:2 1:16 [a] Rev. 1:20; 2:1; 3:1 [b] Is. 49:2 [c] Matt. 17:2 1:17 [a] Ezek. 1:28 [b] Dan. 8:18; 10:10, 12 [c] Is. 41:4; 44:6; 48:12 [1] NU, M omit *to me* 1:18 [a] Rom. 6:9 [b] Ps. 68:20 [1] Lit. *Unseen; the unseen realm* 1:19 [a] Rev. 1:9–18 [b] Rev. 2:1 [c] Rev. 4:1 [1] NU, M *Therefore, write* 1:20 [a] Rev. 2:1 [b] Zech. 4:2 [1] *hidden truth* [2] Or *messengers* [3] NU, M omit *which you saw* 2:1 [a] Rev. 1:16 [b] Rev. 1:13 [1] Or *messenger* 2:2 [a] Ps. 1:6 [b] 1 John 4:1 [c] 2 Cor. 11:13 [1] *perseverance* [2] *endure*

├ LIFE LESSONS ├

■ **1:12, 13**—The seven golden lampstands are seven churches (Rev. 1:20). Jesus is standing in the midst of His churches calling out for repentance—sending out the message of the gospel and offering hope, peace, forgiveness, and redemption to whomever will believe in Him. To live the Christian life is to allow Jesus to live His life in and through us. It is only as He is seen and glorified in us and in our churches that we become effective.

■ **1:17**—Here, the Lord Jesus is clothed as the King, High Priest, Protector, Provider, and Judge of all mankind. The majestic, glorious appearance of the unveiled Christ so overwhelmed John that he fainted. When we stand in His presence at the judgment, we will not be able to say anything. We will see ourselves as He sees us, and we will be in absolute agreement with Him. Therefore, we must live our lives in reverence to Him and never

forget that our Savior and Friend is also our Lord, Master, and Sovereign.

■ **2:2**—We may sometimes feel as though we toil in anonymity and that our labors go unnoticed and unappreciated. However, first we must remember that we do not exist to glorify ourselves but the One who has redeemed us so that others will be saved (Matt. 5:16; John 12:32). Second, we must recall that Jesus notices everything. He sees both our work and the love and obedience we express for Him as we serve (Heb. 6:10). He remembers it all faithfully, and He rewards us when the time is right (1 Cor. 3:11–15; 2 Cor. 5:9, 10; Heb. 11:6).

■ **2:3**—The work Jesus gives us to do can feel taxing and almost unending. To complete our assignment takes both complete reliance upon Him and perseverance. Only when we labor in His strength can we avoid complete weariness (Gal. 6:9).

have persevered and have patience, and have labored for My name's sake and have *a*not become weary. **4**Nevertheless I have *this* against you, that you have left your first love. **5**Remember therefore from where you have fallen; repent and do the first works, *a*or else I will come to you quickly and remove your lampstand from its place—unless you repent. **6**But this you have, that you hate the deeds of the Nicolaitans, which I also hate.

7*a*"He who has an ear, let him hear

2:3 *a* Gal. 6:9 2:5 *a* Matt. 21:41 2:7 *a* Matt. 11:15

LIFE LESSONS

■ **2:4**—How could anything be wrong in a church where people are serving the Lord? Ephesus was a wealthy and influential port city in Asia Minor, which had the potential of becoming a great center for the spread of Christianity. Sadly, the believers there were placing more faith in their earthly riches and works than in the spiritual blessings given to them by the Lord. They were busy *for* Him, but not obedient *to* Him. God created us for an intimate relationship with Himself, and developing that relationship must always remain our top priority. Serving the Lord must be out of obedience—not ritual or tradition—and it must never replace loving Him (1 Sam. 15:22; Jer. 7:23; Hos. 6:6; Mark 12:33).

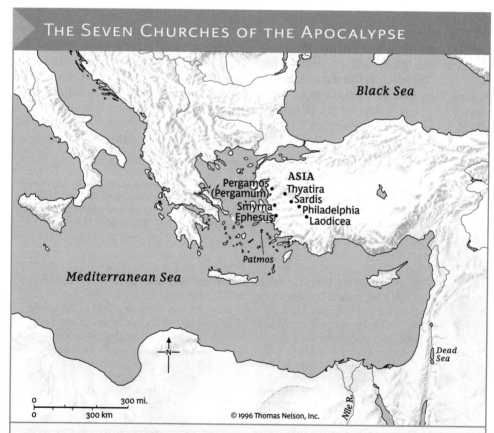

THE SEVEN CHURCHES OF THE APOCALYPSE

Black Sea

ASIA

Pergamos (Pergamum)
•Thyatira
•Sardis
Smyrna•
•Philadelphia
Ephesus•
•Laodicea

Patmos

Mediterranean Sea

Dead Sea

Nile R.

0 ——————— 300 mi.
0 ——————— 300 km   © 1996 Thomas Nelson, Inc.

The churches of seven cities were recipients of an apocalyptic letter from the Lord Jesus through John. By commendation, rebuke, and warning, the people of God were exhorted to remain faithful in adversity. These churches held significant roles in the spread of Christianity in Asia Minor as a result of their location within a transportation network linking different parts of the region.

what the Spirit says to the churches. To him who overcomes I will give *b*to eat from *c*the tree of life, which is in the midst of the Paradise of God.'"

The Persecuted Church

8"And to the *1*angel of the church in Smyrna write,

'These things says *a*the First and the Last, who was dead, and came to life: 9"I know your works, tribulation, and poverty (but you are *a*rich); and *I know* the blasphemy of *b*those who say they are Jews and are not, *c*but *are* a *1*synagogue of Satan. 10*a*Do not fear any of those things which you are about to suffer. Indeed, the devil is about to throw *some* of you into prison, that you may be tested, and you will have tribulation ten days. *b*Be faithful until death, and I will give you *c*the crown of life.

11*a*"He who has an ear, let him hear what the Spirit says to the churches. He who overcomes shall not be hurt by *b*the second death."'

The Compromising Church

12"And to the *1*angel of the church in Pergamos write,

'These things says *a*He who has the sharp two-edged sword: 13"I know your works, and where you dwell, where Satan's throne *is*. And you hold fast to My name, and did not deny My faith even in the days in which Antipas *was* My faithful martyr, who was killed among you, where Satan dwells. 14But I have a few things against you, because you have there those who hold the doctrine of *a*Balaam, who taught Balak to put a stumbling block before the children of Israel, *b*to eat things sacrificed to idols, *c*and to commit sexual immorality. 15Thus you also have those who hold the doctrine of the Nicolaitans, *1*which thing I hate. 16Repent, or else I will come to you quickly and *a*will fight against them with the sword of My mouth.

17"He who has an ear, let him hear what the Spirit says to the churches. To him who overcomes I will give some of the hidden *a*manna to eat. And I will give him a white stone, and on the stone *b*a new name written which no one knows except him who receives *it*."'

The Corrupt Church

18"And to the *1*angel of the church in Thyatira write,

'These things says the Son of God,

2:7 *b* [Rev. 22:2, 14] *c* [Gen. 2:9; 3:22]   2:8 *a* Rev. 1:8, 17, 18 *1* Or *messenger*   2:9 *a* Luke 12:21 *b* Rom. 2:17 *c* Rev. 3:9 *1* congregation   2:10 *a* Matt. 10:22 *b* Matt. 24:13 *c* James 1:12   2:11 *a* Rev. 13:9 *b* [Rev. 20:6, 14; 21:8]   2:12 *a* Rev. 1:16; 2:16 *1* Or *messenger*   2:14 *a* Num. 31:16 *b* Acts 15:29 *c* 1 Cor. 6:13   2:15 *1* NU, M *likewise.*   2:16 *a* 2 Thess. 2:8   2:17 *a* Ex. 16:33, 34 *b* Rev. 3:12   2:18 *1* Or *messenger*

─────────────────────┤ LIFE LESSONS ├─────────────────────

■ **2:9, 10** — The Lord Jesus had nothing negative to say about the church of Smyrna. He understood the persecution they were facing from the "synagogue of Satan"—a group of Jews who were diabolically hostile toward Christians—but He told them that this was for the testing and refinement of their faith. Obedience may bring suffering, but this is because brokenness is God's requirement for maximum usefulness. Sorrows and trials keep us close to the Lord where we can serve Him.

■ **2:13** — The believers at Pergamos dwelt where Satan's throne was because it was a center for worship of many pagan idols, including three Roman Caesars and the four main deities of the Greeks—Zeus, Dionysius, Aesculapius, and Athena. When a believer confessed Christ as Savior and affirmed that there is only one true God, they would incur great persecution and pressure. Yet the Christians at Pergamos refused to renounce their faith in Jesus.

■ **2:14, 15** — Balaam advised the Moabite king, Balak, to defeat Israel by inducing her people to forsake God through sexual iniquity and idolatry (Num. 22–25). The Nicolaitans were a licentious sect who similarly practiced sexual immorality and participated in heathen feasts. Although the believers in Pergamos confessed Christ as their Savior, they had not renounced these pagan practices.

■ **2:16** — No one should ever imagine that because of His unconditional love for us, God will not discipline our unrepentant sinfulness. Jesus uses strong language against those at Pergamos to remind us that He expects us to represent Him well.

[a]who has eyes like a flame of fire, and His feet like fine brass: [19a]"I know your works, love, [1]service, faith, and your [2]patience; and *as* for your works, the last *are* more than the first. [20]Nevertheless I have [1]a few things against you, because you allow [2]that woman [a]Jezebel, who calls herself a prophetess, [3]to teach and seduce My servants [b]to commit sexual immorality and eat things sacrificed to idols. [21]And I gave her time [a]to [1]repent of her sexual immorality, and she did not repent. [22]Indeed I will cast her into a sickbed, and those who commit adultery with her into great tribulation, unless they repent of [1]their deeds. [23]I will kill her children with death, and all the churches shall know that I am He who [a]searches[1] the minds and hearts. And I will give to each one of you according to your works.

[24]"Now to you I say, [1]and to the rest in Thyatira, as many as do not have this doctrine, who have not known the [a]depths of Satan, as they say, [b]I [2]will put on you no other burden. [25]But hold fast [a]what you have till I come. [26]And he who overcomes, and keeps [a]My works until the end, [b]to him I will give power over the nations—

[27] 'He[a] shall rule them with a rod of iron; They shall be dashed to pieces like the potter's vessels'—

as I also have received from My Father; [28]and I will give him [a]the morning star.

[29]"He who has an ear, let him hear what the Spirit says to the churches.'"

The Dead Church

3 "And to the [1]angel of the church in Sardis write,

'These things says He who [a]has the seven Spirits of God and the seven stars: "I know your works, that you have a name that you are alive, but you are dead. [2]Be watchful, and strengthen the things which remain, that are ready to die, for I have not found your works perfect before [1]God. [3a]Remember therefore how you have received and heard; hold fast and [b]repent. [c]Therefore if you will not watch, I will come upon you [d]as a thief, and you will not know what hour I will come upon you. [4][1]You have [a]a few names [2]even in Sardis who have not [b]defiled their garments; and they shall walk with Me [c]in white, for they are worthy. [5]He who overcomes [a]shall be clothed in

2:18 [a]Rev. 1:14, 15 2:19 [a]Rev. 2:2 [1]NU, M *faith, service* [2]*perseverance* 2:20 [a]1 Kin. 16:31; 21:25 [b]Ex. 34:15 [1]NU, M *against you that you tolerate* [2]M *your wife Jezebel* [3]NU, M *and teaches and seduces* 2:21 [a]Rev. 9:20; 16:9, 11 [1]NU, M *repent, and she does not want to repent of her sexual immorality.* 2:22 [1]NU, M *her* 2:23 [a]Jer. 11:20; 17:10 [1]*examines* 2:24 [a]2 Tim. 3:1–9 [b]Acts 15:28 [1]NU, M omit *and* [2]NU, M omit *will* 2:25 [a]Rev. 3:11 2:26 [a][John 6:29] [b][Matt. 19:28] 2:27 [a]Ps. 2:8, 9 2:28 [a]2 Pet. 1:19 3:1 [a]Rev. 1:4, 16 [1]Or *messenger* 3:2 [1]NU, M *My God* 3:3 [a]1 Tim. 6:20 [b]Rev. 3:19 [c]Matt. 24:42, 43 [d][Rev. 16:15] 3:4 [a]Acts 1:15 [b][Jude 23] [c]Rev. 4:4; 6:11 [1]NU, M *Nevertheless you* [2]NU, M omit *even* 3:5 [a][Rev. 19:8]

⊢ LIFE LESSONS ⊢

■ **2:20** — The church at Thyatira allowed a false prophet named Jezebel to lead believers in idolatrous practices and ungodly doctrine. More than likely, this congregation had begun to combine the ideas of the pagan religions in the secular community of Thyatira with their Christian doctrine — a fusion known as *syncretism.*

■ **2:23** — Jesus knows exactly what thoughts we harbor in our minds and hearts — we cannot pretend to be Christians and maintain a belief in other idols. God will not tolerate our divided allegiance. Often, when such duality is found in us, He will allow us to experience trials so we will know that He alone is the Lord and that there is no other.

■ **3:1** — The church at Sardis had a good reputation in the community, but they had lost the power of God — He was no longer being glorified among them. When a congregation loses its connection with God, it often exchanges a personal relationship with God for formalism. This congregation had a superficial form of Christianity, but it did not have an intimate, personal relationship with Jesus Christ (2 Tim. 3:1–7).

■ **3:5** — Those who truly have relationships with the Savior — who do not merely wear their Christianity as a status symbol or offer Him lip service (Matt. 7:21–23) — will be clothed in white, signifying purity, righteousness, and sanctification in Him (Ps. 51:7; Is. 1:18; Rev. 7:14; 19:14). And our names will remain forever in the Lamb's Book of Life (Rev. 20:12–15; 21:27).

white garments, and I will not *b*blot out his name from the *c*Book of Life; but *d*I will confess his name before My Father and before His angels.

6*a*"He who has an ear, let him hear what the Spirit says to the churches."'

The Faithful Church

7"And to the *1*angel of the church in Philadelphia write,

'These things says *a*He who is holy, *b*He who is true, *c*"He who has the key of David, *d*He who opens and no one shuts, and *e*shuts and no one opens": 8*a*"I know your works. See, I have set before you *b*an open door, *1*and no one can shut it; for you have a little strength, have kept My word, and have not denied My name. 9*In-deed I will make *a*those of the synagogue of Satan, who say they are Jews and are not, but lie—indeed *b*I will make them come and worship before your feet, and to know that I have loved you. 10Because you have kept *1*My command to persevere, *a*I also will keep you from the hour of trial which shall come upon *b*the whole world, to test those who dwell *c*on the earth. 11*Behold, *a*I am coming quickly! *b*Hold fast what you have, that no one may take *c*your crown. 12He who overcomes, I will make him *a*a pillar in the temple of My God, and he shall *b*go out no more. *c*I will write on him the name of My God and the name of the city of My

3:5*b*Ex. 32:32　3:5*c*Phil. 4:3　*d*Luke 12:8　3:6*a*Rev. 2:7　3:7*a*Acts 3:14　*b*1 John 5:20　*c*Is. 9:7; 22:22　*d*[Matt. 16:19]　*e*Job 12:14
*1*Or *messenger*　3:8*a*Rev. 3:1　*b*1 Cor. 16:9　*1*NU, M *which no one can shut*　3:9*a*Rev. 2:9　*b*Is. 45:14; 49:23; 60:14
3:10*a*2 Pet. 2:9　*b*Luke 2:1　*c*Is. 24:17　*1*Lit. *the word of My patience*　3:11*a*Phil. 4:5　*b*Rev. 2:25　*c*[Rev. 2:10]
*1*NU, M omit *Behold*　3:12*a*1 Kin. 7:21　*b*Ps. 23:6　*c*[Rev. 14:1; 22:4]

───────────────┤ LIFE LESSONS ├───────────────

■ **3:8** — The church at Philadelphia was a wonderful, faithful church. However, believers there were persecuted by their Jewish brethren who were convinced they — and not Christians — would inherit the kingdom of David (2 Sam. 7:12–16). In fact, in A.D. 90, at the Council of Jamnia, the Jews expelled all believers from the synagogue. Yet Jesus assured them that the door of salvation He opened for them, no one could close (Rom. 8:38, 39). The same is true for us.

■ **3:10** — How do we know that the church of the Lord Jesus Christ will not suffer in the seven-year Tribulation? Because the Lord did not appoint us for wrath, and none of the prophecies concerning the Tribulation in Revelation 4–18 mention the church.

THE SEVEN CHURCHES OF THE APOCALYPSE

	Commendation	Criticism	Instruction	Promise
Ephesus (2:1–7)	Rejects evil, perseveres, has patience	Love for Christ no longer fervent	Do the works you did at first	The tree of life
Smyrna (2:8–11)	Gracefully bears suffering	None	Be faithful until death	The crown of life
Pergamos (2:12–17)	Keeps the faith of Christ	Tolerates immorality, idolatry, and heresies	Repent	Hidden manna and a stone with a new name
Thyatira (2:18–29)	Love, service, faith, patience are greater than at first	Tolerates cult of idolatry and immorality	Judgment coming; keep the faith	Rule over nations and receive morning star
Sardis (3:1–6)	Some have kept the faith	A dead church	Repent; strengthen what remains	Faithful honored and clothed in white
Philadelphia (3:7–13)	Perseveres in the faith, keeps the word of Christ, honors His name	None	Keep the faith	A place in God's presence, a new name, and the New Jerusalem
Laodicea (3:14–22)	None	Indifferent	Be zealous and repent	Share Christ's throne

God, the [d]New Jerusalem, which [e]comes down out of heaven from My God. [f]And *I will write on him* My new name.

[13a]"He who has an ear, let him hear what the Spirit says to the churches."'

The Lukewarm Church

[14]"And to the [1]angel of the church [2]of the Laodiceans write,

[a]"These things says the Amen, [b]the Faithful and True Witness, [c]the Beginning of the creation of God: [15a]"I know your works, that you are neither cold nor hot. I could wish you were cold or hot. [16]So then, because you are lukewarm, and neither [1]cold nor hot, I will vomit you out of My mouth. [17]Because you say, [a]'I am rich, have become wealthy, and have need of nothing'—and do not know that you are wretched, miserable, poor, blind, and naked— [18]I counsel you [a]to buy from Me gold refined in the fire, that you may be rich; and [b]white garments, that you may be clothed, *that* the shame of your nakedness may not be revealed; and anoint your eyes with eye salve, that you may see. [19a]As many as I love, I rebuke and [b]chasten.[1] Therefore be [2]zealous and repent. [20]Behold, [a]I stand at the door and knock. [b]If anyone hears My voice and opens the door, [c]I will come in to him and dine with him, and he with Me. [21]To him who overcomes [a]I will grant to sit with Me on My throne, as I also overcame and sat down with My Father on His throne.

[22a]"He who has an ear, let him hear what the Spirit says to the churches."'"

The Throne Room of Heaven

4 After these things I looked, and behold, a door *standing* [a]open in heaven. And the first voice which I heard *was* like a [b]trumpet speaking with me, saying, "Come up here, and I will show you things which must take place after this."

[2]Immediately [a]I was in the Spirit; and behold, [b]a throne set in heaven, and *One*

3:12 [d] [Heb. 12:22] [e] Rev. 21:2 [f] [Rev. 2:17; 22:4] 3:13 [a] Rev. 2:7 3:14 [a] 2 Cor. 1:20 [b] Rev. 1:5; 3:7; 19:11 [c] [Col. 1:15] [1] Or *messenger* [2] NU, M *in Laodicea* 3:15 [a] Rev. 3:1 3:16 [1] NU, M *hot nor cold* 3:17 [a] Hos. 12:8 3:18 [a] Is. 55:1 [b] 2 Cor. 5:3 3:19 [a] Job 5:17 [b] Heb. 12:6 [1] *discipline* [2] *eager* 3:20 [a] Song 5:2 [b] Luke 12:36, 37 [c] [John 14:23] 3:21 [a] Matt. 19:28 3:22 [a] Rev. 2:7 4:1 [a] Ezek. 1:1 [b] Rev. 1:10 4:2 [a] Rev. 1:10 [b] Is. 6:1

LIFE LESSONS

■ **3:15** — Laodicea was known for its exceptional black wool, medical school, and banking. It was also the picture of ungodly compromise. To illustrate the church's indifferent commitment to Him, Jesus referred to the two sources of water available to them—the icy streams of the Hierapolis and the hot mineral springs to the south. However, once the water reached the city through the six-mile Roman aqueduct, it was tepid and undrinkable. Lukewarm believers who had accommodated secular society had become likewise repellent.

■ **3:16** — Laodicea was a very affluent city, and the believers there were complacent, self-satisfied, and essentially useless to the kingdom of God. They had chosen comfort over spiritual combat and cooperation with the secular culture rather than wholehearted commitment to Jesus Christ. Partial obedience is always disobedience, which is abhorrent to the Lord. And any wealth you hold too tightly in opposition to His will, you will lose.

■ **3:19** — No one likes to be disciplined because it requires a change in perspective, goals, behavior, and attitude. Deeply entrenched sinfulness, compromise, and destructive habits are rooted out, and our earthly sources of security are destroyed. This is all very painful and difficult. But if we cooperate with God when He corrects us, we will become more like Him, and great blessings will always result.

■ **3:20** — Jesus takes the initiative in calling us into a saving relationship with Himself. However, He will not force us to answer. His desire is that we respond to Him in obedience (Luke 12:36). So whenever we feel Him drawing us near to Himself, we should open the door of our lives to Him willingly.

■ **4:1** — From here on, there is no mention of the church on earth until the Second Coming of Christ, and there is a reason for it. Only *tribulation saints*—people who accept Jesus as their Savior after the Rapture—are present during this time of suffering and judgment. The church is not present for the wrath (1 Thess. 5:9). Rather, the church is caught up in the air to be with Him (1 Cor. 15:51–57; 1 Thess. 4:15–17).

sat on the throne. [31]And He who sat there was [a]like a jasper and a sardius stone in appearance; [b]and *there was* a rainbow around the throne, in appearance like an emerald. [4][a]Around the throne *were* twenty-four thrones, and on the thrones I saw twenty-four elders sitting, [b]clothed in white [1]robes; and they had crowns of gold on their heads. [5]And from the throne proceeded [a]lightnings, [1]thunderings, and voices. [b]Seven lamps of fire *were* burning before the throne, which are [c]the[2] seven Spirits of God.

[6]Before the throne *there* [1]*was* [a]a sea of glass, like crystal. [b]And in the midst of the throne, and around the throne, *were* four living creatures full of eyes in front and in back. [7][a]The first living creature *was* like a lion, the second living creature like a calf, the third living creature had a face like a man, and the fourth living creature *was* like a flying eagle. [8]*The* four living creatures, each having [a]six wings, were full of eyes around and within. And they do not rest day or night, saying:

[b]"Holy,[1] holy, holy,
    [c]Lord God Almighty,
        [d]Who was and is and is to come!"

[9]Whenever the living creatures give glory and honor and thanks to Him who sits on the throne, [a]who lives forever and ever, [10][a]the twenty-four elders fall down before Him who sits on the throne and worship Him who lives forever and ever, and cast their crowns before the throne, saying:

[11] "You[a] are worthy, [1]O Lord,
    To receive glory and
        honor and power;
    [b]For You created all things,
    And by [c]Your will they [2]exist
        and were created."

The Lamb Takes the Scroll

5 And I saw in the right *hand* of Him who sat on the throne [a]a scroll written inside and on the back, [b]sealed with seven seals. [2]Then I saw a strong angel proclaiming with a loud voice, [a]"Who is worthy to open the scroll and to loose its seals?" [3]And no one in heaven or on the earth or under the earth was able to open the scroll, or to look at it.

[4]So I wept much, because no one was found worthy to open [1]and read the scroll, or to look at it. [5]But one of the elders said

4:3 [a] Rev. 21:11   [b] Ezek. 1:28   [1] M omits *And He who sat there was*, making the following a description of the throne.   4:4 [a] Rev. 11:16   [b] Rev. 3:4, 5   [1] NU, M *robes, with crowns*   4:5 [a] Rev. 8:5; 11:19; 16:18   [b] Ezek. 37:23   [c] [Rev. 1:4]   [1] NU, M *voices, and thunderings.* [2] M omits *the*   4:6 [a] Rev. 15:2   [b] Ezek. 1:5   [1] NU, M add *something like*   4:7 [a] Ezek. 1:10; 10:14   4:8 [a] Is. 6:2   [b] Is. 6:3   [c] Rev. 1:8   [d] Rev. 1:4   [1] M has *holy* nine times.   4:9 [a] Rev. 1:18   4:10 [a] Rev. 5:8, 14; 7:11; 11:16; 19:4   4:11 [a] Rev. 1:6; 5:12   [b] Gen. 1:1   [c] Col. 1:16   [1] NU, M *our Lord and God*   [2] NU, M *existed*   5:1 [a] Ezek. 2:9, 10   [b] Is. 29:11   5:2 [a] Rev. 4:11; 5:9   5:4 [1] NU, M omit *and read*

⊢ LIFE LESSONS ⊢

■ **4:5** — As John looks upon the Lord's throne in heaven, he realizes that he is witnessing what will occur when God's judgment comes — as shown by the lightning and thunder. He also sees the seven spirits, who are a symbol of the Holy Spirit (Is. 11:2) and who demonstrate that the Lord's wrath is perfectly informed and from a faultless perspective.

■ **4:8** — This is the theme of the Book of Revelation: God rules the earth and every individual in it on the basis of His eternal holiness and perfect judgment. He evaluates every situation and can tell us what is coming because He inhabits eternity — existing from the infinite past and forever without end. No one is like Him, and only He is worthy of praise.

■ **4:11** — As our Creator, God is worthy of all praise and adoration. We are merely a reflection

of His glory. This will be abundantly clear when we all reach heaven. All who know the Lord — who have seen Him in all of His beauty, holiness, power, and majesty — will worship Him and lay our crowns at His feet in thankfulness, giving Him the glory and honor He deserves.

■ **5:4** — Who is worthy to hold eternal life and everlasting condemnation in His hands? The fifth chapter of Revelation reveals that no other leader, religious figure, or ruler in history could open this important scroll about God's righteous judgment. Only one Person — the risen Savior, who sacrificed Himself for all mankind — could open it. Jesus is unique and superior to all.

■ **5:5** — This is true for us in *every* situation because Jesus prevails when no one else can. As the Lamb of God (1 Cor. 5:7), He took our sins upon

to me, "Do not weep. Behold, [a]the Lion of the tribe of [b]Judah, [c]the Root of David, has [d]prevailed to open the scroll [e]and [1]to loose its seven seals."

[6]And I looked, [1]and behold, in the midst of the throne and of the four living creatures, and in the midst of the elders, stood [a]a Lamb as though it had been slain, having seven horns and [b]seven eyes, which are [c]the seven Spirits of God sent out into all the earth. [7]Then He came and took the scroll out of the right hand [a]of Him who sat on the throne.

Worthy Is the Lamb

[8]Now when He had taken the scroll, [a]the four living creatures and the twenty-four elders fell down before the Lamb, each having a harp, and golden bowls full of incense, which are the [b]prayers of the saints. [9]And [a]they sang a new song, saying:

[b]"You are worthy to take the scroll,
　And to open its seals;
　For You were slain,
　And [c]have redeemed us to
　　God [d]by Your blood
　Out of every tribe and tongue
　　and people and nation,
[10]　And have made [1]us [a]kings[2]
　　and [b]priests to our God;
　And [3]we shall reign on the earth."

[11]Then I looked, and I heard the voice of many angels around the throne, the living creatures, and the elders; and the number of them was ten thousand times ten thousand, and thousands of thousands, [12]saying with a loud voice:

"Worthy is the Lamb who was slain
To receive power and
　riches and wisdom,
And strength and honor and
　glory and blessing!"

[13]And [a]every creature which is in heaven and on the earth and under the earth and such as are in the sea, and all that are in them, I heard saying:

[b]"Blessing and honor and
　glory and power
Be to Him [c]who sits on the throne,
And to the Lamb, forever and [1]
　ever!"

[14]Then the four living creatures said, "Amen!" And the [1]twenty-four elders fell down and worshiped [2]Him who lives forever and ever.

First Seal: The Conqueror

6 Now [a]I saw when the Lamb opened one of the [1]seals; and I heard [b]one of the four living creatures saying with a voice like thunder, "Come and see."

5:5 [a]Gen. 49:9　[b]Heb. 7:14　[c]Is. 11:1, 10　[d]Rev. 3:21　[e]Rev. 6:1　[1]NU, M omit *to loose*　5:6 [a][John 1:29]　[b]Zech. 3:9; 4:10　[c]Rev. 1:4; 3:1; 4:5　[1]NU, M *I saw in the midst . . . a Lamb standing*　5:7 [a]Rev. 4:2　5:8 [a]Rev. 4:8–10; 19:4　[b]Rev. 8:3　5:9 [a]Rev. 14:3　[b]Rev. 4:11　[c]John 1:29　[d][Heb. 9:12]　5:10 [a]Ex. 19:6　[b]Is. 61:6　[1]NU, M *them*　[2]NU *a kingdom*　[3]NU, M *they*　5:13 [a]Phil. 2:10　[b]1 Chr. 29:11　[c]Rev. 4:2, 3; 6:16; 20:11　[1]M adds *Amen*　5:14 [1]NU, M omit *twenty-four*　[2]NU, M omit *Him who lives forever and ever*　6:1 [a][Rev. 5:5–7, 12; 13:8]　[b]Rev. 4:7　[1]NU, M *seven seals*

⊢　LIFE LESSONS　⊢

Himself, giving His life on the cross so we could be saved. As the Lion of Judah (Gen. 49:9, 10; Hos. 5:14, 15), He is coming as the conquering warrior and Messiah who will bring justice to the earth. Finally, as the Root of David (Is. 11:1–10; Rom. 15:12; Rev. 22:16, 17), Jesus fulfills the promises made to King David and ushers in His everlasting kingdom (2 Sam. 7:10–16).

■ 5:9 —God does not play favorites. He offers His gift of salvation to people from every ethnic group, race, and language from throughout the world. He is truly the God of all the earth. And in heaven, there will be people from every tribe, tongue, and nation as evidence of it.

■ 5:13 —As the moment nears for the Lamb to break open the seven seals of the judgment, all creation worships Him (Is. 45:23; Rom. 14:11; Phil. 2:10, 11). Here we can see the unity of the Godhead—both the Father and Son are worshiped as One. He is the sovereign King of the universe. He is our Creator and deserves all our praise.

[2]And I looked, and behold, [a]a white horse. [b]He who sat on it had a bow; [c]and a crown was given to him, and he went out [d]conquering and to conquer.

Second Seal: Conflict on Earth

[3]When He opened the second seal, [a]I heard the second living creature saying, "Come [1]and see." [4a]Another horse, fiery red, went out. And it was granted to the one who sat on it to [b]take peace from the earth, and that *people* should kill one another; and there was given to him a great sword.

Third Seal: Scarcity on Earth

[5]When He opened the third seal, [a]I heard the third living creature say, "Come and see." So I looked, and behold, [b]a black horse, and he who sat on it had a pair of [c]scales[1] in his hand. [6]And I heard a voice in the midst of the four living creatures saying, "A [1]quart of wheat for a [2]denarius, and three quarts of barley for a denarius; and [a]do not harm the oil and the wine."

Fourth Seal: Widespread Death on Earth

[7]When He opened the fourth seal, [a]I heard the voice of the fourth living creature saying, "Come and see." [8a]So I looked, and behold, a pale horse. And the name of him who sat on it was Death, and Hades followed with him. And [1]power was given to them over a fourth of the earth, [b]to kill with sword, with hunger, with death, [c]and by the beasts of the earth.

Fifth Seal: The Cry of the Martyrs

[9]When He opened the fifth seal, I saw under [a]the altar [b]the souls of those who had been slain [c]for the word of God and for [d]the testimony which they held. [10]And they cried with a loud voice, saying, [a]"How long, O Lord, [b]holy and true, [c]until You judge and avenge our blood on those who dwell on the earth?" [11]Then a [a]white robe was given to each of them; and it was said to them [b]that they should rest a little while longer, until both *the number of* their fellow servants and their brethren, who would be killed as they *were,* was completed.

Sixth Seal: Cosmic Disturbances

[12]I looked when He opened the sixth seal, [a]and [1]behold, there was a great earthquake; and [b]the sun became black

6:2 [a] Zech. 1:8; 6:3 [b] Ps. 45:4, 5, LXX [c] Zech. 6:11 [d] Matt. 24:5   6:3 [a] Rev. 4:7 [1] NU, M omit *and see*   6:4 [a] Zech. 1:8; 6:2 [b] Matt. 24:6, 7 6:5 [a] Rev. 4:7 [b] Zech. 6:2, 6 [c] Matt. 24:7 [1] *balances*   6:6 [a] Rev. 7:3; 9:4 [1] Gr. *choinix,* about 1 quart [2] About 1 day's wage for a worker 6:7 [a] Rev. 4:7   6:8 [a] Zech. 6:3 [b] Ezek. 5:12, 17; 14:21; 29:5 [c] Lev. 26:22 [1] *authority*   6:9 [a] Rev. 8:3 [b] [Rev. 20:4] [c] Rev. 1:2, 9 [d] 2 Tim. 1:8 6:10 [a] Zech. 1:12 [b] Rev. 3:7 [c] Rev. 11:18   6:11 [a] Rev. 3:4, 5; 7:9 [b] Heb. 11:40   6:12 [a] Matt. 24:7 [b] Joel 2:10, 31; 3:15 [1] NU, M omit *behold*

⊢ **LIFE LESSONS** ⊢

■ **6:2** — When the Lamb breaks the first seal of judgment, the Antichrist appears on the scene with deceptive answers for the woes of the world, and he is catapulted into a place of authority (2 Thess. 2:3–12; 1 John 2:22). He leads the world in opposition to God. Through him, the Lord tests what is really in people's hearts.

■ **6:4** — When the red horse is released, war will break out in ways that we have never seen before. War is seen as an instrument of God's judgment throughout the Old Testament (Ezek. 21). Romans 1:28, 29 explains, "As they did not like to retain God in their knowledge, God gave them over to a debased mind . . . being filled with all unrighteousness, sexual immorality, wickedness, covetousness, maliciousness; full of envy, murder, strife, deceit, evil-mindedness; they are whisperers."

■ **6:5** — The black horse represents what normally follows war — famine and poverty. Economies and crops will be destroyed, and people all over the earth will suffer terrible hunger.

■ **6:8** — The pale horse, Death, is given power over a fourth of the earth's population — more people than any of us can imagine. However, this is so the three-fourths of the world who remain will realize their sinfulness, repent, and accept Christ.

■ **6:9** — This is not a reference to the church, but to tribulation saints. After the Rapture, there will be those who realize that believers were right — Jesus Christ *is* the only Savior — and they will accept His salvation. They will preach the gospel, and many people will be saved because of their testimony. However, they will also face great persecution. God will not forget them, but He will wait until everything He has promised is complete before He honors them.

as sackcloth of hair, and the [2]moon became like blood. [13a]And the stars of heaven fell to the earth, as a fig tree drops its late figs when it is shaken by a mighty wind. [14a]Then the sky [1]receded as a scroll when it is rolled up, and [b]every mountain and island was moved out of its place. [15]And the [a]kings of the earth, the great men, [1]the rich men, the commanders, the mighty men, every slave and every free man, [b]hid themselves in the caves and in the rocks of the mountains, [16a]and said to the mountains and rocks, "Fall on us and hide us from the face of Him who [b]sits on the throne and from the wrath of the Lamb! [17]For the great day of His wrath has come, [a]and who is able to stand?"

The Sealed of Israel

7 After these things I saw four angels standing at the four corners of the earth, [a]holding the four winds of the earth, [b]that the wind should not blow on the earth, on the sea, or on any tree. [2]Then I saw another angel ascending from the east, having the seal of the living God. And he cried with a loud voice to the four angels to whom it was granted to harm the earth and the sea, [3]saying, [a]"Do not harm the earth, the sea, or the trees till we have sealed the servants of our God [b]on their foreheads." [4a]And I heard the number of those who were sealed. [b]One hundred and forty-four thousand [c]of all the tribes of the children of Israel were sealed:

5 of the tribe of Judah
    twelve thousand were sealed;
 of the tribe of Reuben
    twelve thousand were [1]sealed;
 of the tribe of Gad
    twelve thousand were sealed;
6 of the tribe of Asher
    twelve thousand were sealed;
 of the tribe of Naphtali
    twelve thousand were sealed;
 of the tribe of Manasseh
    twelve thousand were sealed;
7 of the tribe of Simeon
    twelve thousand were sealed;
 of the tribe of Levi
    twelve thousand were sealed;
 of the tribe of Issachar
    twelve thousand were sealed;
8 of the tribe of Zebulun
    twelve thousand were sealed;
 of the tribe of Joseph
    twelve thousand were sealed;
 of the tribe of Benjamin
    twelve thousand were sealed.

A Multitude from the Great Tribulation

[9]After these things I looked, and behold, [a]a great multitude which no one could number, [b]of all nations, tribes, peoples,

6:12 [2]NU, M *whole moon*   6:13 [a]Rev. 8:10; 9:1   6:14 [a]Is. 34:4   [b]Rev. 16:20   [1]Or *split apart*   6:15 [a]Ps. 2:2–4   [b]Is. 2:10, 19, 21; 24:21   [1]NU, M *the commanders, the rich men,*   6:16 [a]Luke 23:29, 30   [b]Rev. 20:11   6:17 [a]Zeph. 1:14   7:1 [a]Dan. 7:2   [b]Rev. 7:3; 8:7; 9:4   7:3 [a]Rev. 6:6   [b]Rev. 22:4   7:4 [a]Rev. 9:16   [b]Rev. 14:1, 3   [c]Gen. 49:1–27   7:5 [1]NU, M omit *sealed* in vv. 5b–8b.   7:9 [a]Rom. 11:25   [b]Rev. 5:9

LIFE LESSONS

■ **6:17**—Note that it is the ungodly who make this statement. They recognize God's hand in their circumstances, and yet they refuse to repent. Judgment always results when people refuse to humble themselves before the Lord. Yet they will find in that day that neither wealth nor power nor social connections will be able to save them. Though they cling to these things for safety, in the day of the Lord, all will turn to ashes.
■ **7:3**—God marks His children with a permanent seal that shows we belong to Him (Ezek. 9:4–6; 2 Cor. 1:22; Eph. 1:13; 4:30). During the last days, this will be revealed by a mark on the forehead, which distinguishes believers from those who have completely rejected the Lord and those who worship the Antichrist (Rev. 13:15–17; 14:1–5).
■ **7:4**—These 144,000 people from the tribes of Israel are messianic Jews who will go throughout the world sharing the gospel and leading people into a growing relationship with Jesus Christ. God's promise of salvation to believers does not negate or replace His love for the nation of Israel (Rom. 11). On the contrary, here we see how He is once again trying to bring His people into a right relationship with Himself.
■ **7:9**—God redeems multitudes of people from every nation, culture, and background (Matt. 24:14). His grace reaches into every corner of the

and tongues, standing before the throne and before the Lamb, *c*clothed with white robes, with palm branches in their hands, [10]and crying out with a loud voice, saying, *a*"Salvation *belongs* to our God *b*who sits on the throne, and to the Lamb!" [11]*a*All the angels stood around the throne and the elders and the four living creatures, and fell on their faces before the throne and *b*worshiped God, [12]*a*saying:

"Amen! Blessing and glory and wisdom,
    Thanksgiving and honor
        and power and might,
Be to our God forever and ever.
Amen."

[13]Then one of the elders answered, saying to me, "Who are these arrayed in *a*white robes, and where did they come from?"

[14]And I said to him, *1*"Sir, you know."

So he said to me, *a*"These are the ones who come out of the great tribulation, and *b*washed their robes and made them white in the blood of the Lamb. [15]Therefore they are before the throne of God, and serve

Him day and night in His temple. And He who sits on the throne will *a*dwell among them. [16]*a*They shall neither hunger anymore nor thirst anymore; *b*the sun shall not strike them, nor any heat; [17]for the Lamb who is in the midst of the throne *a*will shepherd them and lead them to *1*living fountains of waters. *b*And God will wipe away every tear from their eyes."

Seventh Seal: Prelude to the Seven Trumpets

8 When*a* He opened the seventh seal, there was silence in heaven for about half an hour. [2]*a*And I saw the seven angels who stand before God, *b*and to them were given seven trumpets. [3]Then another angel, having a golden censer, came and stood at the altar. He was given much incense, that he should offer *it* with *a*the prayers of all the saints upon *b*the golden altar which was before the throne. [4]And *a*the smoke of the incense, with the prayers of the saints, ascended before God from the angel's hand. [5]Then the angel took the censer, filled it with fire from the altar, and threw *it* to the

---

7:9 *c* Rev. 3:5, 18; 4:4; 6:11   7:10 *a* Ps. 3:8   *b* Rev. 5:13   7:11 *a* Rev. 4:6   *b* Rev. 4:11; 5:9, 12, 14; 11:16   7:12 *a* Rev. 5:13, 14   7:13 *a* Rev. 7:9
7:14 *a* Rev. 6:9   *b* [Heb. 9:14]   *1* NU, M *My lord*   7:15 *a* Is. 4:5, 6   7:16 *a* Is. 49:10   *b* Ps. 121:6   7:17 *a* Ps. 23:1   *b* Rev. 21:4
1 NU, M *fountains of the waters of life*   8:1 *a* Rev. 6:1   8:2 *a* [Matt. 18:10]   *b* 2 Chr. 29:25–28
8:3 *a* Rev. 5:8   *b* Ex. 30:1   8:4 *a* Ps. 141:2

⊢ LIFE LESSONS ⊢

world, and His salvation is offered to everyone (2 Pet. 3:9).

■ **7:14**—This multitude of tribulation saints did not accept the gospel before the church was taken up to heaven (1 Cor. 15:51–57; 1 Thess. 4:15–17). However, some time after the Rapture, they understood the truth and received Jesus Christ as their Lord and Savior. The blood of the Lamb takes away our sin and makes us pure and holy when we believe in Him (Is. 1:18; Heb. 9:14; 1 John 1:7).

■ **7:17**—This world is filled with pain and suffering—especially for the tribulation saints, who endure God's judgment on the world and the persecution of the Antichrist. But in heaven there is no more pain, hunger, sorrow, or fear. God will wipe away any remnant of tears in our eyes from our difficulties here on earth (Is. 25:8; Matt. 5:4; Rev. 21:4). "In Your presence is fullness of joy; at Your right hand are pleasures forevermore" (Ps. 16:11).

■ **8:1**—Every creature in heaven watching God's

plan unfold is so absolutely awed about what is happening there is dead silence. No one speaks. No song is sung. Everyone waits in hushed reverence for the Lord's next pronouncement—the seven trumpet judgments. Some of God's works are so overwhelming that the only appropriate response is reverent silence. "The LORD is in His holy temple. Let all the earth keep silence before Him" (Hab. 2:20).

■ **8:4**—It is awe-inspiring to think that the silence of heaven is also in honor of the prayers of the tribulation saints for comfort, deliverance, vindication, and justice. The Father accepts the prayers of His faithful people as fragrant sacrifices—offerings that honor Him. In prayer, we admit our weakness and declare our trust in His wisdom and strength.

■ **8:5**—The angel takes the same censer that carried the prayers of the saints and throws it back to earth with God's answer—judgment on earth. And *a*there were noises, thunderings, *b*lightnings, *c*and an earthquake.

6So the seven angels who had the seven trumpets prepared themselves to sound.

First Trumpet: Vegetation Struck

7The first angel sounded: *a*And hail and fire followed, mingled with blood, and they were thrown *b*to the *1*earth. And a third *c*of the trees were burned up, and all green grass was burned up.

Second Trumpet: The Seas Struck

8Then the second angel sounded: *a*And *something* like a great mountain burning with fire was thrown into the sea, *b*and a third of the sea *c*became blood. 9*a*And a third of the living creatures in the sea died, and a third of the ships were destroyed.

Third Trumpet: The Waters Struck

10Then the third angel sounded: *a*And a great star fell from heaven, burning like a torch, *b*and it fell on a third of the rivers and on the springs of water. 11*a*The name of the star is Wormwood. *b*A third of the waters became wormwood, and many men died from the water, because it was made bitter.

Fourth Trumpet: The Heavens Struck

12*a*Then the fourth angel sounded: And a third of the sun was struck, a third of the moon, and a third of the stars, so that a third of them were darkened. A third of the day *1*did not shine, and likewise the night.

13And I looked, *a*and I heard an *1*angel flying through the midst of heaven, saying with a loud voice, *b*"Woe, woe, woe to the inhabitants of the earth, because of the remaining blasts of the trumpet of the three angels who are about to sound!"

Fifth Trumpet: The Locusts from the Bottomless Pit

9 Then the fifth angel sounded: *a*And I saw a star fallen from heaven to the earth. To him was given the key to *b*the *1*bottomless pit. 2And he opened the bottomless pit, and smoke arose out of the pit like the smoke of a great furnace. So the *a*sun and the air were darkened because of the smoke of the pit. 3Then out of the smoke locusts came upon the earth. And to them was given power, *a*as the scorpions of the earth have power. 4They were commanded *a*not to harm *b*the grass of the earth, or any green thing, or any tree, but only those men who do not have *c*the seal of God on their foreheads. 5And *1*they were not given *authority* to kill them, *a*but to torment them *for* five months. Their torment *was* like the torment of a scorpion when it strikes a man. 6In those days *a*men will seek

8:5 *a* Rev. 11:19; 16:18 *b* Rev. 4:5 *c* 2 Sam. 22:8   8:7 *a* Ezek. 38:22 *b* Rev. 16:2 *c* Rev. 9:4, 15–18 *1* NU, M add *and a third of the earth was burned up*   8:8 *a* Jer. 51:25 *b* Ex. 7:17 *c* Ezek. 14:19   8:9 *a* Rev. 16:3   8:10 *a* Is. 14:12 *b* Rev. 14:7; 16:4   8:11 *a* Ruth 1:20 *b* Ex. 15:23   8:12 *a* Is. 13:10 *1* *had no light*   8:13 *a* Rev. 14:6; 19:17 *b* Rev. 9:12; 11:14; 12:12 *1* NU, M *eagle*   9:1 *a* Rev. 8:10 *b* Luke 8:31 *1* Lit. *shaft of the abyss*   9:2 *a* Joel 2:2, 10   9:3 *a* Judg. 7:12   9:4 *a* Rev. 6:6 *b* Rev. 8:7 *c* Rev. 7:2, 3   9:5 *a* [Rev. 9:10; 11:7] *1* The locusts   9:6 *a* Jer. 8:3

⊦   LIFE LESSONS   ⊦

the wicked. This is why we stand tallest and strongest on our knees because the Lord answers our prayers in ways that are beyond imagination.

■ **8:13** — The judgments described in Revelation grow in intensity and scale as time progresses. God typically employs escalating judgments to prompt repentance—at every turn He demonstrates that He is the Lord and there is no other (Ex. 9:14; Deut. 4:35, 39; 32:39; Is. 43:10–12; 44:6–8; 45:5–7). He eliminates everything that people are dependent upon in the hope that they will repent, believe in Jesus Christ, and be saved (Ezek. 18:32; John 3:16–18; 2 Pet. 3:9).

■ **9:4** — The locusts are only permitted to torment servants of the Antichrist—they are not permitted to touch the people of God. Just as the Lord protected the Israelites from many of His plagues against Pharaoh (Ex. 8:22; 9:6, 26; 10:23; 12:27), He safeguards His people from many of the judgments against the wicked during the Tribulation.

death and will not find it; they will desire to die, and death will flee from them.

7[a]The shape of the locusts was like horses prepared for battle. [b]On their heads were crowns of something like gold, [c]and their faces *were* like the faces of men. 8They had hair like women's hair, and [a]their teeth were like lions' *teeth.* 9And they had breastplates like breastplates of iron, and the sound of their wings *was* [a]like the sound of chariots with many horses running into battle. 10They had tails like scorpions, and there were stings in their tails. Their power *was* to hurt men five months. 11And they had as king over them [a]the angel of the bottomless pit, whose name in Hebrew *is* [1]Abaddon, but in Greek he has the name [2]Apollyon.

12[a]One woe is past. Behold, still two more woes are coming after these things.

Sixth Trumpet: The Angels from the Euphrates

13Then the sixth angel sounded: And I heard a voice from the four horns of the [a]golden altar which is before God, 14saying to the sixth angel who had the trumpet, "Release the four angels who are bound [a]at the great river Euphrates." 15So the four angels, who had been prepared

for the hour and day and month and year, were released to kill a [a]third of mankind. 16Now [a]the number of the army [b]of the horsemen *was* two hundred million; [c]I heard the number of them. 17And thus I saw the horses in the vision: those who sat on them had breastplates of fiery red, hyacinth blue, and sulfur yellow; [a]and the heads of the horses *were* like the heads of lions; and out of their mouths came fire, smoke, and brimstone. 18By these three *plagues* a third of mankind was killed—by the fire and the smoke and the brimstone which came out of their mouths. 19For [1]their power is in their mouth and in their tails; [a]for their tails *are* like serpents, having heads; and with them they do harm.

20But the rest of mankind, who were not killed by these plagues, [a]did not repent of the works of their hands, that they should not worship [b]demons, [c]and idols of gold, silver, brass, stone, and wood, which can neither see nor hear nor walk. 21And they did not repent of their murders [a]or their [1]sorceries or their sexual immorality or their thefts.

The Mighty Angel with the Little Book

10 I saw still another mighty angel coming down from heaven, clothed with a cloud. [a]And a rainbow

9:7[a]Joel 2:4 [b]Nah. 3:17 [c]Dan. 7:8   9:8[a]Joel 1:6   9:9[a]Joel 2:5–7   9:11[a]Eph. 2:2 [1]Lit. *Destruction* [2]Lit. *Destroyer*   9:12[a]Rev. 8:13; 11:14   9:13[a]Rev. 8:3   9:14[a]Rev. 16:12   9:15[a]Rev. 8:7–9; 9:18   9:16[a]Dan. 7:10 [b]Ezek. 38:4 [c]Rev. 7:4   9:17[a]Is. 5:28, 29   9:19[a]Is. 9:15 [1]NU, M *the power of the horses*   9:20[a]Deut. 31:29 [b]1 Cor. 10:20 [c]Dan. 5:23   9:21[a]Rev. 21:8; 22:15 [1]NU, M *drugs*   10:1[a]Rev. 4:3

⊢ LIFE LESSONS ⊢

■ 9:6 — Jesus said, "Whoever desires to save his life will lose it, but whoever loses his life for My sake will find it" (Matt. 16:25). Many people refuse to believe in Christ because they do not want to give up control of their lives. However, anything we hold too tightly, we will lose. In the end times, people will despair of the lives they've fought so hard to keep. God does not desire for anyone to perish, so He will use even severe pain to get our attention and urge us back to Him.

■ 9:15 — Despite the chaos on earth that the Book of Revelation describes, God remains completely in control (Ps. 103:19). The Lord has prepared these angels for this specific work at this

precise time. Likewise, God has chosen the particular circumstances, era, location, and giftedness with which you exist for the purpose of serving Him. And the awareness of His presence in your situation can energize you for your work if you will trust Him.

■ 9:20 — Why does the Book of Revelation repeatedly tell us that the wicked did not repent? First, because it shows the necessity of God's judgment. Second, because it shows the Lord's desire that every person repent and live (Ezek. 18:32; 2 Pet. 3:9). Yet their hearts are so hardened against God that instead of repenting, their rebellion intensifies (Prov. 28:14; Lam. 3:64–66; John 12:37–43; Rom. 1:18–32; Eph. 4:18, 19).

was on *b*his head, his face *was* like the sun, and *c*his feet like pillars of fire. ²He had a little book open in his hand. *a*And he set his right foot on the sea and *his* left *foot* on the land, ³and cried with a loud voice, as *when* a lion roars. When he cried out, *a*seven thunders uttered their voices. ⁴Now when the seven thunders *ᴵ*uttered their voices, I was about to write; but I heard a voice from heaven saying ²to me, *a*"Seal up the things which the seven thunders uttered, and do not write them."

⁵The angel whom I saw standing on the sea and on the land *a*raised up his *ᴵ*hand to heaven ⁶and swore by Him who lives forever and ever, *a*who created heaven and the things that are in it, the earth and the things that are in it, and the sea and the things that are in it, *b*that there should be delay no longer, ⁷but *a*in the days of the sounding of the seventh angel, when he is about to sound, the mystery of God would be finished, as He declared to His servants the prophets.

John Eats the Little Book

⁸Then the voice which I heard from heaven spoke to me again and said, "Go, take the little book which is open in the hand of the angel who stands on the sea and on the earth."

⁹So I went to the angel and said to him, "Give me the little book."

And he said to me, *a*"Take and eat it; and it will make your stomach bitter, but it will be as sweet as honey in your mouth."

¹⁰Then I took the little book out of the angel's hand and ate it, *a*and it was as sweet as honey in my mouth. But when I had eaten it, *b*my stomach became bitter. ¹¹And *ᴵ*he said to me, "You must prophesy again about many peoples, nations, tongues, and kings."

The Two Witnesses

11 Then I was given *a*a reed like a measuring rod. *ᴵ*And the angel stood, saying, *b*"Rise and measure the temple of God, the altar, and those who worship there. ²But leave out *a*the court which is outside the temple, and do not measure it, *b*for it has been given to the Gentiles. And they will *c*tread the holy city underfoot *for* *d*forty-two months. ³And I will give *power* to my two *a*witnesses, *b*and they will prophesy *c*one thousand two hundred and sixty days, clothed in sackcloth."

⁴These are the *a*two olive trees and the two lampstands standing before the *ᴵ*God of the earth. ⁵And if anyone wants to harm them, *a*fire proceeds from their mouth and devours their enemies. *b*And

10:1*b* Rev. 1:16　*c* Rev. 1:15　10:2*a* Matt. 28:18　10:3*a* Ps. 29:3–9　10:4*a* Dan. 8:26; 12:4, 9　*ᴵ* NU, M *sounded,*　²NU, M omit *to me*　10:5*a* Dan. 12:7　*ᴵ* NU, M *right hand*　10:6*a* Rev. 4:11　*b* Rev. 16:17　10:7*a* Rev. 11:15　10:9*a* Jer. 15:16　10:10*a* Ezek. 3:3　*b* Ezek. 2:10　10:11*ᴵ* NU, M *they*　11:1*a* Ezek. 40:3–42:20　*b* Num. 23:18　*ᴵ* NU, M omit *And the angel stood*　11:2*a* Ezek. 40:17, 20　*b* Ps. 79:1　*c* Dan. 8:10　*d* Rev. 12:6; 13:5　11:3*a* Rev. 20:4　*b* Rev. 19:10　*c* Rev. 12:6　11:4*a* Zech. 4:2, 3, 11, 14　*ᴵ* NU, M *Lord*　11:5*a* 2 Kin. 1:10–12　*b* Num. 16:29

⊢ LIFE LESSONS ⊢

■ **10:4** — God reveals to us the things He wants us to know. He does not disclose details about the future to satisfy our curiosity, but to motivate and equip us to live for Him today with passion, holiness, and joy. He also leaves some particulars unknown so we will cling to Him and seek Him for wisdom and direction.

■ **10:7** — God will move heaven and earth to show us His will, and throughout history, He has spoken to us about what will take place through His prophets (1 Pet. 1:10–13). However, we may not fully understand it all until it is fulfilled, just as the disciples did not comprehend all the

prophecies concerning Jesus until they saw Him as the resurrected Messiah (John 2:19–22; 12:12–16).

■ **10:9** — It is always a joy to read and proclaim the Word of God. Yet some parts of Scripture — like these passages describing catastrophic divine judgment — give no pleasure either to the prophets or to the Lord (Jer. 15:16, 17, 19; Ezek. 2:8 — 3:15). We partake of God's Word for our own edification, but once we read it, we also have a responsibility of warning others of what is to come if they do not repent and believe in the Lord Jesus.

if anyone wants to harm them, he must be killed in this manner. 6These *a*have power to shut heaven, so that no rain falls in the days of their prophecy; and they have power over waters to turn them to blood, and to strike the earth with all plagues, as often as they desire.

The Witnesses Killed

7When they *a*finish their testimony, *b*the beast that ascends *c*out of the bottomless pit *d*will make war against them, overcome them, and kill them. 8And their dead bodies *will lie* in the street of *a*the great city which spiritually is called Sodom and Egypt, *b*where also *1*our Lord was crucified. 9*a*Then *those* from the peoples, tribes, tongues, and nations *1*will see their dead bodies three-and-a-half days, *b*and not allow their dead bodies to be put into graves. 10*a*And those who dwell on the earth will rejoice over them, make merry, *b*and send gifts to one another, *c*because these two prophets tormented those who dwell on the earth.

The Witnesses Resurrected

11*a*Now after the three-and-a-half days *b*the breath of life from God entered them, and they stood on their feet, and great fear fell on those who saw them. 12And *1*they heard a loud voice from heaven saying to them, "Come up here." *a*And they ascended to heaven *b*in a cloud, *c*and their enemies saw them. 13In the same hour *a*there was a great earthquake, *b*and a tenth of the city fell. In the earthquake seven thousand people were killed, and the rest were afraid *c*and gave glory to the God of heaven.

14*a*The second woe is past. Behold, the third woe is coming quickly.

Seventh Trumpet: The Kingdom Proclaimed

15Then *a*the seventh angel sounded: *b*And there were loud voices in heaven, saying, *c*"The *1*kingdoms of this world have become *the kingdoms* of our Lord and of His Christ, *d*and He shall reign forever and ever!" 16And *a*the twenty-four elders who sat before God on their thrones fell on their faces and *b*worshiped God, 17saying:

"We give You thanks, O Lord
    God Almighty,
The One *a*who is and who was
    *1*and who is to come,
Because You have taken Your
    great power *b*and reigned.
18 The nations were *a*angry, and
        Your *1*wrath has come,
    And the time of the *b*dead, that
        they should be judged,
    And that You should reward
        Your servants the prophets
        and the saints,

11:6 *a*1 Kin. 17:1   11:7 *a*Luke 13:32   *b*Rev. 13:1, 11; 17:8   *c*Rev. 9:1, 2   *d*Dan. 7:21   11:8 *a*Rev. 14:8   *b*Heb. 13:12   *1*NU, M *their*   11:9 *a*Rev. 17:15   *b*Ps. 79:2, 3   *1*NU, M *see . . . and will not allow*   11:10 *a*Rev. 12:12   *b*Esth. 9:19, 22   *c*Rev. 16:10   11:11 *a*Rev. 11:9   *b*Ezek. 37:5, 9, 10   11:12 *a*Is. 14:13   *b*Acts 1:9   *c*2 Kin. 2:11, 12   *1*M *I*   11:13 *a*Rev. 6:12; 8:5; 11:19; 16:18   *b*Rev. 16:19   *c*Rev. 14:7; 16:9; 19:7   11:14 *a*Rev. 8:13; 9:12   11:15 *a*Rev. 8:2; 10:7   *b*Is. 27:13   *c*Rev. 12:10   *d*Ex. 15:18   *1*NU, M *kingdom . . . has become the kingdom*   11:16 *a*Rev. 4:4   *b*Rev. 4:11; 5:9, 12, 14; 7:11   11:17 *a*Rev. 16:5   *b*Rev. 19:6   *1*NU, M *omit and who is to come*   11:18 *a*Ps. 2:1   *b*Dan. 7:10   *1*anger

---

┤ LIFE LESSONS ├

■ **11:6** —The miracles described here may remind us of the wonders performed through Elijah (1 Kin. 17:1) and Moses (Ex. 7:14—12:42). The same God who empowered them will demonstrate His power once again so that many can be saved.
■ **11:7** —We will not leave this earth until the Father deems fit (Luke 12:6–8; 21:17–19). The two witnesses described here cannot be touched by their enemies until they have completed every task assigned to them by God.
■ **11:13** —This is the only time in Revelation that a tragedy prompts those who survive to give glory to God. Tragedies such as this devastating earthquake are terrible, but the Lord can use them to show people their great need for His grace and redemption.
■ **11:15** —The time is coming when every inch of this planet will be illuminated by the glory of our King, the Lord Jesus Christ. "The earth shall be full of the knowledge of the LORD as the waters cover the sea" (Is. 11:9). He reigns triumphantly over the world forever.

And those who fear Your
name, small and great,
And should destroy those
who destroy the earth."

¹⁹Then ᵃthe temple of God was opened in heaven, and the ark of ¹His covenant was seen in His temple. And ᵇthere were lightnings, noises, thunderings, an earthquake, ᶜand great hail.

The Woman, the Child, and the Dragon

12 Now a great sign appeared in heaven: a woman clothed with the sun, with the moon under her feet, and on her head a garland of twelve stars. ²Then being with child, she cried out ᵃin labor and in pain to give birth.

³And another sign appeared in heaven: behold, ᵃa great, fiery red dragon having seven heads and ten horns, and seven diadems on his heads. ⁴ᵃHis tail drew a third ᵇof the stars of heaven ᶜand threw them to the earth. And the dragon stood ᵈbefore the woman who was ready to give birth, ᵉto devour her Child as soon as it was born. ⁵She bore a male Child

ᵃwho was to rule all nations with a rod of iron. And her Child was ᵇcaught up to God and His throne. ⁶Then ᵃthe woman fled into the wilderness, where she has a place prepared by God, that they should feed her there ᵇone thousand two hundred and sixty days.

Satan Thrown Out of Heaven

⁷And war broke out in heaven: ᵃMichael and his angels fought ᵇwith the dragon; and the dragon and his angels fought, ⁸but they ¹did not prevail, nor was a place found for ²them in heaven any longer. ⁹So ᵃthe great dragon was cast out, ᵇthat serpent of old, called the Devil and Satan, ᶜwho deceives the whole world; ᵈhe was cast to the earth, and his angels were cast out with him.

¹⁰Then I heard a loud voice saying in heaven, ᵃ"Now salvation, and strength, and the kingdom of our God, and the power of His Christ have come, for the accuser of our brethren, ᵇwho accused them before our God day and night, has been cast down. ¹¹And ᵃthey overcame him by the blood of the Lamb and by the

11:19 ᵃRev. 4:1; 15:5, 8 ᵇRev. 8:5 ᶜRev. 16:21 ¹M the covenant of the Lord 12:2 ᵃIs. 26:17; 66:6–9 12:3 ᵃRev. 13:1; 17:3, 7, 9 12:4 ᵃRev. 9:10, 19 ᵇRev. 8:7, 12 ᶜDan. 8:10 ᵈRev. 12:2 ᵉMatt. 2:16 12:5 ᵃPs. 2:9 ᵇActs 1:9–11 12:6 ᵃRev. 12:4, 14 ᵇRev. 11:3; 13:5 12:7 ᵃDan. 10:13, 21; 12:1 ᵇRev. 20:2 12:8 ¹were not strong enough ²M him 12:9 ᵃJohn 12:31 ᵇGen. 3:1, 4 ᶜRev. 20:3 ᵈRev. 9:1 12:10 ᵃRev. 11:15 ᵇZech. 3:1 12:11 ᵃRom. 16:20

⊢   LIFE LESSONS   ⊢

■ **11:19**—The ark of the covenant symbolized God's relationship with Israel (Ex. 25:22). It normally remained in the Most Holy Place, and His presence would appear above it—making it one of the most sacred articles of Israel's worship. Yet the ark had not been seen in Israel since the destruction of the first temple in 586 B.C. (2 Kin. 25:8, 9). Here, we see the ark is kept safely in the Lord's care—His sign to Israel that He will honor His covenants with them (Gen. 12:1–3; 2 Sam. 7:12–16) and that His provision of salvation is for them as well.

■ **12:4**—Some believe the stars represent angels and that the Enemy convinced a third of them to rebel against God. The devil's goal is to divert us from an intimate relationship with the Lord God, and he has the power to do terrible evil in our lives, so we must resist him and stand firm in our faith (1 Pet. 5:9).

■ **12:9**—The devil fell from his lofty position in the Lord's kingdom because of pride—he

wanted to make himself "like the Most High" (Is. 14:14). Yet God has always been and will forever be superior to the Enemy. The Lord triumphs over evil and will ultimately send the Adversary to everlasting condemnation (Rev. 20:10).

■ **12:10**—Romans 8:34 tells us, "Who is he who condemns? It is Christ who died, and furthermore is also risen, who is even at the right hand of God, who also makes intercession for us." No one has a right to bring any condemnation against those who have trusted in Christ as their Savior, because the Lord Jesus Himself testifies on our behalf (Rom. 8:1). And at the right time, Jesus will rid us forever of the Enemy who has tempted and tormented us.

■ **12:11**—We cannot win our battles against Satan with swords, bullets, or bombs (2 Cor. 10:3–6; Eph. 6:10–18). Rather, our invincible weapons are salvation through Christ and the Word of God. When we accept Jesus Christ as our Savior, the devil's ability to destroy our souls is removed

word of their testimony, *b*and they did not love their lives to the death. ¹²Therefore *a*rejoice, O heavens, and you who dwell in them! *b*Woe to the inhabitants of the earth and the sea! For the devil has come down to you, having great wrath, *c*because he knows that he has a short time."

The Woman Persecuted

¹³Now when the dragon saw that he had been cast to the earth, he persecuted *a*the woman who gave birth to the male *Child.* ¹⁴*a*But the woman was given two wings of a great eagle, *b*that she might fly *c*into the wilderness to her place, where she is nourished *d*for a time and times and half a time, from the presence of the serpent. ¹⁵So the serpent *a*spewed water out of his mouth like a flood after the woman, that she might cause her to be carried away by the flood. ¹⁶But the earth helped the woman, and the earth opened its mouth and swallowed up the flood which the dragon had spewed out of his mouth. ¹⁷And the dragon was enraged with the woman, and he went to make war with the rest of her offspring, who keep the commandments of God and have the testimony of Jesus ¹Christ.

The Beast from the Sea

13 Then ¹I stood on the sand of the sea. And I saw *a*a beast rising up out of the sea, *b*having ²seven heads and ten horns, and on his horns ten crowns, and on his heads a *c*blasphemous name. ²Now the beast which I saw was like a leopard, his feet were like *the feet of* a bear, and his mouth like the mouth of a lion. The *a*dragon gave him his power, his throne, and great authority. ³And I saw one of his heads *a*as if it had been mortally wounded, and his deadly wound was healed. And *b*all the world marveled and followed the beast. ⁴So they worshiped the dragon who gave authority to the beast; and they worshiped the beast, saying, *a*"Who *is* like the beast? Who is able to make war with him?"

⁵And he was given *a*a mouth speaking great things and blasphemies, and he was given authority to ¹continue for *b*forty-two months. ⁶Then he opened his mouth in blasphemy against God, to blaspheme His name, *a*His tabernacle, and those who dwell in heaven. ⁷It was granted to him *a*to make war with the saints and to overcome them. And *b*authority was given him over every ¹tribe, tongue, and nation. ⁸All who dwell on the

---

12:11*b*Luke 14:26 12:12*a*Ps. 96:11 *b*Rev. 8:13 *c*Rev. 10:6 12:13*a*Rev. 12:5 12:14*a*Ex. 19:4 *b*Rev. 12:6 *c*Rev. 17:3 *d*Dan. 7:25; 12:7
12:15*a*Is. 59:19 12:17¹NU, M omit *Christ* 13:1*a*Dan. 7:2, 7 *b*Rev. 12:3 *c*Rev. 17:3 ¹NU *he* ²NU, M *ten horns and seven heads*
13:2*a*Rev. 12:3, 9; 13:4, 12 13:3*a*Rev. 13:12, 14 *b*Rev. 17:8 13:4*a*Rev. 18:18 13:5*a*Dan. 7:8, 11, 20, 25; 11:36 *b*Rev. 11:2
¹M *make war* 13:6*a*[Col. 2:9] 13:7*a*Dan. 7:21 *b*Rev. 11:18 ¹NU, M add *and people*

├   LIFE LESSONS   ├

(John 10:27–30). So he goes to work in other ways, seeking to hinder our effectiveness for the kingdom of God. This is why we must obey what the Lord teaches us through His Word. The principles in His Word are anchors that keep us steady in times of storm (Prov. 30:5; Rom. 15:4; 2 Tim. 3:16, 17; Heb. 4:12; 1 Pet. 1:22–25).

■ **13:3** — The Beast — or Antichrist — will attempt to deceive the world by staging a false resurrection. However, only the Lord Jesus Christ can give eternal life. Though the Enemy will counterfeit Christ's work, he will never be able to escape the everlasting condemnation that awaits him (Rev. 20:10). Neither will *anyone* who rejects Jesus (vv. 11–15).

■ **13:5** — The Beast opposes the Lord and tries to destroy all that He loves, and no horror in history will compare with the Antichrist's reign of terror.

However, the Beast's time is short — God will strictly control the length of his rule, and even what he can do. The Lord remains sovereign, regardless of all the Enemy does.

■ **13:7** — Why will God allow the Antichrist to harm His people? Jesus said, "Unless a grain of wheat falls into the ground and dies, it remains alone; but if it dies, it produces much grain" (John 12:24). Through the saints' faithful example, even in the face of death, others will know Christ as Savior.

■ **13:8** — Before the foundation of the world, God created us with free will so we could choose to love and obey Him. Knowing sin would enter the world, He prepared a plan of salvation that includes eternal forgiveness, redemption, and reconciliation. All of this was provided for at the

earth will worship him, [a]whose names have not been written in the Book of Life of the Lamb slain [b]from the foundation of the world.

9[a]If anyone has an ear, let him hear. 10[a]He who leads into captivity shall go into captivity; [b]he who kills with the sword must be killed with the sword. [c]Here is the [1]patience and the faith of the saints.

The Beast from the Earth

11Then I saw another beast [a]coming up out of the earth, and he had two horns like a lamb and spoke like a dragon. 12And he exercises all the authority of the first beast in his presence, and causes the earth and those who dwell in it to worship the first beast, [a]whose deadly wound was healed. 13[a]He performs great signs, [b]so that he even makes fire come down from heaven on the earth in the sight of men. 14[a]And he deceives [1]those who dwell on the earth [b]by those signs which he was granted to do in the sight of the beast, telling those who dwell on the earth to make an image to the beast who was wounded by the sword [c]and lived. 15He was granted *power* to give breath to the image of the beast, that the image of the beast should both speak [a]and cause as many as would not worship the image of the beast to be killed. 16He causes all, both small and great, rich and poor, free and slave, [a]to receive a mark on their right hand or on their foreheads, 17and that no one may buy or sell except one who has [1]the mark or [a]the name of the beast, [b]or the number of his name.

18[a]Here is wisdom. Let him who has [b]understanding calculate [c]the number of the beast, [d]for it is the number of a man: His number *is* 666.

The Lamb and the 144,000

14 Then I looked, and behold, [1]a [a]Lamb standing on Mount Zion, and with Him [b]one hundred *and* forty-four thousand, 2having His Father's name [c]written on their foreheads. 2And I heard a voice from heaven, [a]like the voice of many waters, and like the voice of loud thunder. And I heard the sound of [b]harpists playing their harps. 3They sang as it were a new song before the throne, before the four living creatures, and the elders; and no one could learn that song [a]except the hundred *and* forty-four thousand who were redeemed from the earth. 4These are the ones who were not defiled with women, [a]for they are virgins. These are the ones [b]who follow the Lamb wherever He goes. These [c]were [1]redeemed from *among* men, [d]*being* firstfruits to God and to the Lamb. 5And [a]in their mouth was found no [1]deceit, for [b]they are without fault [2]before the throne of God.

13:8 [a] Ex. 32:32   [b] Rev. 17:8   13:9 [a] Rev. 2:7   13:10 [a] Is. 33:1   [b] Gen. 9:6   [c] Rev. 14:12   [1] *perseverance*   13:11 [a] Rev. 11:7   13:12 [a] Rev. 13:3, 4
13:13 [a] Matt. 24:24   [b] 1 Kin. 18:38   13:14 [a] Rev. 12:9   [b] 2 Thess. 2:9   [c] 2 Kin. 20:7   [1] M *my own people*   13:15 [a] Rev. 16:2   13:16 [a] Rev. 7:3;
14:9; 20:4   13:17 [a] Rev. 14:9–11   [b] Rev. 15:2   [1] NU, M *the mark, the name*   13:18 [a] Rev. 17:9   [b] [1 Cor. 2:14]   [c] Rev. 15:2   [d] Rev. 21:17
14:1 [a] Rev. 5:6   [b] Rev. 7:4; 14:3   [c] Rev. 7:3; 22:4   [1] NU, M *the*   [2] NU, M add *His name and*   14:2 [a] Rev. 1:15; 19:6   [b] Rev. 5:8
14:3 [a] Rev. 5:9   14:4 [a] [2 Cor. 11:2]   [b] Rev. 3:4; 7:17   [c] Rev. 5:9   [d] James 1:18   [1] M adds *by Jesus*   14:5 [a] Ps. 32:2
[b] Eph. 5:27   [1] NU, M *falsehood*   [2] NU, M omit the rest of v. 5.

⊢   LIFE LESSONS   ⊢

Cross. In the last days, the beast will manipulate the lost by counterfeiting God's work and tricking them into worshiping him. But those who know the Lord Jesus as their Savior will not be deceived by the Enemy.

■ **13:11** — This second beast is the false prophet. Along with the dragon, which is Satan, and the first Beast, which is the Antichrist, these three form an evil triumvirate that opposes God.

■ **13:16** — In Revelation 7:3, God marks His children with a permanent seal, showing we belong to Him. This seal appears as people accept Christ as their Savior. However, the beast *forces* the remaining people to take his mark just to buy and sell goods. Those who accept the beast's mark submit themselves to his ownership forever.

■ **14:1** — While the Tribulation is occurring on earth, the Lord Jesus stands triumphantly on Mount Zion — which is the heavenly Jerusalem. With Him are the 144,000 missionaries who faithfully proclaimed the gospel (Rev. 7:3–8).

The Proclamations of Three Angels

⁶Then I saw another angel ᵃflying in the midst of heaven, ᵇhaving the everlasting gospel to preach to those who dwell on the earth—ᶜto every nation, tribe, tongue, and people— ⁷saying with a loud voice, ᵃ"Fear God and give glory to Him, for the hour of His judgment has come; ᵇand worship Him who made heaven and earth, the sea and springs of water."

⁸And another angel followed, saying, ᵃ"Babylon¹ is fallen, is fallen, that great city, because ᵇshe has made all nations drink of the wine of the wrath of her fornication."

⁹Then a third angel followed them, saying with a loud voice, ᵃ"If anyone worships the beast and his image, and receives his ᵇmark on his forehead or on his hand, ¹⁰he himself ᵃshall also drink of the wine of the wrath of God, which is ᵇpoured out full strength into ᶜthe cup of His indignation. ᵈHe shall be tormented with ᵉfire and brimstone in the presence of the holy angels and in the presence of the Lamb. ¹¹And ᵃthe smoke of their torment ascends forever and ever; and they have no rest day or night, who worship the beast and his image, and whoever receives the mark of his name."

¹²ᵃHere is the ¹patience of the saints; ᵇhere² are those who keep the commandments of God and the faith of Jesus.

¹³Then I heard a voice from heaven saying ¹to me, "Write: ᵃ'Blessed are the dead ᵇwho die in the Lord from now on.'"

"Yes," says the Spirit, ᶜ"that they may rest from their labors, and their works follow ᵈthem."

Reaping the Earth's Harvest

¹⁴Then I looked, and behold, a white cloud, and on the cloud sat One like the Son of Man, having on His head a golden crown, and in His hand a sharp sickle. ¹⁵And another angel ᵃcame out of the temple, crying with a loud voice to Him who sat on the cloud, ᵇ"Thrust in Your sickle and reap, for the time has come ¹for You to reap, for the harvest ᶜof the earth is ripe." ¹⁶So He who sat on the cloud thrust in His sickle on the earth, and the earth was reaped.

Reaping the Grapes of Wrath

¹⁷Then another angel came out of the temple which is in heaven, he also having a sharp sickle.

¹⁸And another angel came out from the altar, ᵃwho had power over fire, and he cried with a loud cry to him who had the sharp sickle, saying, ᵇ"Thrust in your sharp sickle and gather the clusters of the vine of the earth, for her grapes are fully ripe." ¹⁹So the angel thrust his sickle into the earth and gathered the vine of the earth, and threw it into ᵃthe great winepress of the wrath of God. ²⁰And ᵃthe winepress was trampled ᵇoutside

14:6 ᵃ Rev. 8:13 ᵇ Eph. 3:9 ᶜ Rev. 13:7 14:7 ᵃ Rev. 11:18 ᵇ Neh. 9:6 14:8 ᵃ Is. 21:9 ᵇ Jer. 51:7 ¹ NU Babylon the great is fallen,
is fallen, which has made; M Babylon the great is fallen. 14:9 ᵃ Rev. 13:14, 15; 14:11 ᵇ Rev. 13:16
14:10 ᵃ Ps. 75:8 ᵇ Rev. 18:6 ᶜ Rev. 16:19 ᵈ Rev. 20:10 ᵉ 2 Thess. 1:7 14:11 ᵃ Is. 34:8–10 14:12 ᵃ Rev. 13:10 ᵇ Rev. 12:17
¹ steadfastness, perseverance ² NU, M omit here are those 14:13 ᵃ Eccl. 4:1, 2 ᵇ 1 Cor. 15:18 ᶜ Heb. 4:9, 10
ᵈ [1 Cor. 3:11–15; 15:58] ¹ NU, M omit to me 14:15 ᵃ Rev. 16:17 ᵇ Joel 3:13 ᶜ Jer. 51:33 ¹ NU, M omit for You
14:18 ᵃ Rev. 16:8 ᵇ Joel 3:13 14:19 ᵃ Rev. 19:15 14:20 ᵃ Is. 63:3 ᵇ Heb. 13:12

LIFE LESSONS

■ 14:7 — Three angels arrive with three final messages of warning. The first proclaims the gospel. The second declares the demise of the Beast's kingdom. The third warns that God's wrath is near for whomever has received the mark of the Beast. The Lord's judgment is about to begin, but because He wants all to be saved, He continues to call unbelievers to repentance (Ezek. 18:32; John 3:16–18; 2 Pet. 3:9).

■ 14:11 — Hell is a place of eternal suffering — the unredeemed souls of the lost are forever separated from God, the only One who could have made them whole (Rev. 20:15). "'There is no peace,' says the Lᴏʀᴅ, 'for the wicked'" (Is. 48:22).

■ 14:15 — Jesus will send His angels to separate the wheat from the tares — the godly from the wicked — just as He said He would (Matt. 13:24–30, 36–43).

the city, and blood came out of the winepress, ^cup to the horses' bridles, for one thousand six hundred ¹furlongs.

Prelude to the Bowl Judgments

15 Then ^aI saw another sign in heaven, great and marvelous: ^bseven angels having the seven last plagues, ^cfor in them the wrath of God is complete.

²And I saw *something* like ^aa sea of glass ^bmingled with fire, and those who have the victory over the beast, ^cover his image and ¹over his mark *and* over the ^dnumber of his name, standing on the sea of glass, ^ehaving harps of God. ³They sing ^athe song of Moses, the servant of God, and the song of the ^bLamb, saying:

^c"Great and marvelous *are* Your works,
    Lord God Almighty!
^dJust and true *are* Your ways,
    O King of the ¹saints!
4 ^aWho shall not fear You, O Lord,
    and glorify Your name?
For *You* alone *are* ^bholy.
For ^call nations shall come
    and worship before You,
For Your judgments have
    been manifested."

⁵After these things I looked, and ¹behold, ^athe ²temple of the tabernacle of the testimony in heaven was opened.

⁶And out of the ¹temple came the seven angels having the seven plagues, ^aclothed in pure bright linen, and having their chests girded with golden bands. ⁷^aThen one of the four living creatures gave to the seven angels seven golden bowls full of the wrath of God ^bwho lives forever and ever. ⁸^aThe temple was filled with smoke ^bfrom the glory of God and from His power, and no one was able to enter the temple till the seven plagues of the seven angels were completed.

16 Then I heard a loud voice from the temple saying ^ato the seven angels, "Go and pour out the ¹bowls ^bof the wrath of God on the earth."

First Bowl: Loathsome Sores

²So the first went and poured out his bowl ^aupon the earth, and a ¹foul and ^bloathsome sore came upon the men ^cwho had the mark of the beast and those ^dwho worshiped his image.

Second Bowl: The Sea Turns to Blood

³Then the second angel poured out his bowl ^aon the sea, and ^bit became blood as of a dead *man;* ^cand every living creature in the sea died.

Third Bowl: The Waters Turn to Blood

⁴Then the third angel poured out his bowl ^aon the rivers and springs of water,

---

14:20 ^cIs. 34:3 ¹Lit. *stadia,* about 184 miles in all   15:1 ^aRev. 12:1, 3   ^bRev. 21:9   ^cRev. 14:10   15:2 ^aRev. 4:6   ^b[Matt. 3:11]   ^cRev. 13:14, 15   ^dRev. 13:17   ^eRev. 5:8   ¹NU, M omit *over his mark*   15:3 ^aEx. 15:1–21   ^bRev. 15:3   ^cDeut. 32:3, 4   ^dPs. 145:17   ¹NU, M *nations*   15:4 ^aEx. 15:14   ^bLev. 11:44   ^cIs. 66:23   15:5 ^aNum. 1:50   ¹NU, M omit *behold*   ²*sanctuary,* the inner shrine   15:6 ^aEx. 28:6   ¹*sanctuary,* the inner shrine   15:7 ^aRev. 4:6   ^b1 Thess. 1:9   15:8 ^aEx. 19:18; 40:34   ^b2 Thess. 1:9   16:1 ^aRev. 15:1   ^bRev. 14:10   ¹NU, M *seven bowls*   16:2 ^aRev. 8:7   ^bEx. 9:9–11   ^cRev. 13:15–17; 14:9   ^dRev. 13:14   ¹*severe and malignant,* lit. *bad and evil*   16:3 ^aRev. 8:8; 11:6   ^bEx. 7:17–21   ^cRev. 8:9   16:4 ^aRev. 8:10

⊢   LIFE LESSONS   ⊢

■ **15:4**—One day, every knee shall bow and every tongue confess that Jesus is Lord (Rom. 14:11; Phil. 2:10). Some will prostrate themselves willingly before Him out of love, joy, worship, and respect. Others will bend their knee to Him out of dread. But everyone *will* bow.

■ **15:8**—Whenever God unveils His full majesty and holiness, His splendor overwhelms the stoutest heart, and worship is the result. This happened with Isaiah (Is. 6:4, 5) and at the dedications of both the tabernacle (Ex. 40:34, 35) and the

temple in Jerusalem (1 Kin. 8:10, 11). This will be especially true during the time of judgment when His astounding power and righteousness are shown throughout the earth.

■ **16:2**—God has complete and utter control over the entire earth—the waters (Rev. 16:3, 4), the sun (v. 8), and every element of creation (Job 38:4 — 41:34; Ps. 103:19; Luke 8:25). From these seven bowls of wrath come the last and worst of all the judgments.

[b]and they became blood. [5]And I heard the angel of the waters saying:

[a]"You are righteous, [1]O Lord,
The One [b]who is and who
[2]was and who is to be,
Because You have judged these things.
6 For [a]they have shed the blood
[b]of saints and prophets,
[c]And You have given them
blood to drink.
[1]For it is their just due."

[7]And I heard [1]another from the altar saying, "Even so, [a]Lord God Almighty, [b]true and righteous *are* Your judgments."

Fourth Bowl: Men Are Scorched

[8]Then the fourth angel poured out his bowl [a]on the sun, [b]and power was given to him to scorch men with fire. [9]And men were scorched with great heat, and they [a]blasphemed the name of God who has power over these plagues; [b]and they did not repent [c]and give Him glory.

Fifth Bowl: Darkness and Pain

[10]Then the fifth angel poured out his bowl [a]on the throne of the beast, [b]and his kingdom became full of darkness; [c]and they gnawed their tongues because of the pain. [11]They blasphemed the God of heaven because of their pains and their sores, and did not repent of their deeds.

Sixth Bowl: Euphrates Dried Up

[12]Then the sixth angel poured out his bowl [a]on the great river Euphrates, [b]and its water was dried up, [c]so that the way of the kings from the east might be prepared. [13]And I saw three unclean [a]spirits like frogs *coming* out of the mouth of [b]the dragon, out of the mouth of the beast, and out of the mouth of [c]the false prophet. [14]For they are spirits of demons, [a]performing signs, *which* go out to the kings [1]of the earth and of [b]the whole world, to gather them to [c]the battle of that great day of God Almighty.

[15a]"Behold, I am coming as a thief. Blessed *is* he who watches, and keeps his garments, [b]lest he walk naked and they see his shame."

[16a]And they gathered them together to the place called in Hebrew, [1]Armageddon.

Seventh Bowl: The Earth Utterly Shaken

[17]Then the seventh angel poured out his bowl into the air, and a loud voice came out of the temple of heaven, from the throne, saying, [a]"It is done!" [18]And [a]there were noises and thunderings and lightnings; [b]and there was a great earthquake, such a mighty and great earthquake [c]as had not occurred since men were on the earth. [19]Now [a]the great city was divided into three parts, and the cities of the nations fell. And [b]great Babylon [c]was remembered before God, [d]to give her the cup of the wine of the fierceness of His wrath. [20]Then [a]every island fled away, and the mountains were not found. [21]And great hail from heaven fell upon men, *each hailstone* about the weight of a talent. Men blasphemed God

16:4 [b] Ex. 7:17–20   16:5 [a] Rev. 15:3, 4   [b] Rev. 1:4, 8   [1] NU, M omit O Lord   [2] NU, M *was, the Holy One*   16:6 [a] Matt. 23:34   [b] Rev. 11:18   [c] Is. 49:26   [1] NU, M omit *For*   16:7 [a] Rev. 15:3   [b] Rev. 13:10; 19:2   [1] NU, M omit *another from*   16:8 [a] Rev. 8:12   [b] Rev. 9:17, 18   16:9 [a] Rev. 16:11   [b] Dan. 5:22   [c] Rev. 11:13   16:10 [a] Rev. 13:2   [b] Rev. 8:12; 9:2   [c] Rev. 11:10   16:12 [a] Rev. 9:14   [b] Jer. 50:38   [c] Is. 41:2, 25; 46:11   16:13 [a] 1 John 4:1   [b] Rev. 12:3, 9   [c] Rev. 13:11, 14; 19:20; 20:10   16:14 [a] 2 Thess. 2:9   [b] Luke 2:1   [c] Rev. 17:14; 19:19; 20:8   [1] NU, M omit *of the earth and*   16:15 [a] Matt. 24:43   [b] 2 Cor. 5:3   16:16 [a] Rev. 19:19   [1] Lit. *Mount Megiddo*; M *Megiddo*   16:17 [a] Rev. 10:6; 21:6   16:18 [a] Rev. 4:5   [b] Rev. 11:13   [c] Dan. 12:1   16:19 [a] Rev. 14:8   [b] Rev. 17:5, 18   [c] Rev. 14:8; 18:5   [d] Is. 51:17   16:20 [a] Rev. 6:14; 20:11

LIFE LESSONS

■ **16:15** — We must be ready for Christ's return, *whenever* He comes back. We are to remain faithful, completing whatever tasks He gives us, so that "we may have confidence and not be ashamed before Him at His coming" (1 John 2:28).
■ **16:16** — This is the plain of Megiddo, which is on a strategic highway between Egypt and Mesopotamia. It is here that the kings and armies of the world gather for their war against Jerusalem, where they will fight the Lord Jesus in the last great battle before He begins His millennial reign (Rev. 19:11 — 20:6).

because of the plague of the hail, since that plague was exceedingly great.

The Scarlet Woman and the Scarlet Beast

17 Then [a]one of the seven angels who had the seven bowls came and talked with me, saying [1]to me, "Come, [b]I will show you the judgment of [c]the great harlot [d]who sits on many waters, [2a]with whom the kings of the earth committed fornication, and [b]the inhabitants of the earth were made drunk with the wine of her fornication."

[3]So he carried me away in the Spirit [a]into the wilderness. And I saw a woman sitting [b]on a scarlet beast *which was* full of [c]names of blasphemy, having seven heads and ten horns. [4]The woman [a]was arrayed in purple and scarlet, [b]and adorned with gold and precious stones and pearls, [c]having in her hand a golden cup [d]full of abominations and the filthiness of [1]her fornication. [5]And on her forehead a name *was* written:

[a]MYSTERY, BABYLON THE GREAT,
THE MOTHER OF HARLOTS
AND OF THE ABOMINATIONS
OF THE EARTH.

[6]I saw [a]the woman, drunk [b]with the blood of the saints and with the blood of [c]the martyrs of Jesus. And when I saw her, I marveled with great amazement.

The Meaning of the Woman and the Beast

[7]But the angel said to me, "Why did you marvel? I will tell you the [1]mystery of the woman and of the beast that carries her, which has the seven heads and the ten horns. [8]The beast that you saw was, and is not, and [a]will ascend out of the bottomless pit and [b]go to [1]perdition. And those who [c]dwell on the earth [d]will marvel, [e]whose names are not written in the Book of Life from the foundation of the world, when they see the beast that was, and is not, and [2]yet is.

[9a]"Here *is* the mind which has wisdom: [b]The seven heads are seven mountains on which the woman sits. [10]There are also seven kings. Five have fallen, one is, *and* the other has not yet come. And when he comes, he must [a]continue a short time. [11]The [a]beast that was, and is not, is himself also the eighth, and is of the seven, and is going to [1]perdition.

[12a]"The ten horns which you saw are ten kings who have received no kingdom as yet, but they receive authority for one hour as kings with the beast. [13]These are of one mind, and they will give their power and authority to the beast. [14a]These will make war with the Lamb,

17:1 [a]Rev. 1:1; 21:9 [b]Rev. 16:19 [c]Nah. 3:4 [d]Jer. 51:13 [1]NU, M omit *to me*   17:2 [a]Rev. 2:22; 18:3, 9 [b]Jer. 51:7   17:3 [a]Rev. 12:6, 14; 21:10 [b]Rev. 12:3 [c]Rev. 13:1   17:4 [a]Rev. 18:12, 16 [b]Dan. 11:38 [c]Jer. 51:7 [d]Rev. 14:8 [1]M *the fornication of the earth*   17:5 [a]2 Thess. 2:7   17:6 [a]Rev. 18:24 [b]Rev. 13:15 [c]Rev. 6:9, 10   17:7 [1]*hidden truth*   17:8 [a]Rev. 11:7 [b]Rev. 13:10; 17:11 [c]Rev. 3:10 [d]Rev. 13:3 [e]Rev. 13:8 [1]*destruction* [2]NU, M *shall be present*   17:9 [a]Rev. 13:18 [b]Rev. 13:1   17:10 [a]Rev. 13:5 17:11 [a]Rev. 13:3, 12, 14; 17:8 [1]*destruction*   17:12 [a]Dan. 7:20   17:14 [a]Rev. 16:14; 19:19

⊢   LIFE LESSONS   ⊢

■ **17:1, 2** —The great harlot is the apostate church—people who claim to be religious and observe seemingly pious rituals, but who never accept Jesus Christ as their Savior. These are the cults that pervert who Christ is and what He has done for us. They are false religions that add requirements for salvation or deny Him altogether. The idolatrous church is often employed by a government to control the populace. After believers are gathered to the Lord in the Rapture, the apostate church will continue to exist and will be used as a pawn by the Antichrist.

■ **17:6** —The apostate church persecutes believers in Christ with a murderous vengeance, completely intolerant of the truth. There are a great many more Christian martyrs today than there were even in the days of the early church. And as we draw closer to the end times, that number is sure to increase worldwide.

■ **17:14** —These kings will ultimately do battle with the Lord at His Second Coming (Rev. 19:19–21). It is always foolish for anyone to think that they can openly oppose the sovereign Lord of the universe or those He loves. However, this is exactly what the kings who follow the beast will do. And they will be soundly defeated for all eternity (Rev. 20:10–15).

and the Lamb will [b]overcome them, [c]for He is Lord of lords and King of kings; [d]and those *who are* with Him *are* called, chosen, and faithful."

[15]Then he said to me, [a]"The waters which you saw, where the harlot sits, [b]are peoples, multitudes, nations, and tongues. [16]And the ten horns which you [1]saw on the beast, [a]these will hate the harlot, make her [b]desolate [c]and naked, eat her flesh and [d]burn her with fire. [17a]For God has put it into their hearts to fulfill His purpose, to be of one mind, and to give their kingdom to the beast, [b]until the words of God are fulfilled. [18]And the woman whom you saw [a]is that great city [b]which reigns over the kings of the earth."

The Fall of Babylon the Great

18 After[a] these things I saw another angel coming down from heaven, having great authority, [b]and the earth was illuminated with his glory. [2]And he cried [1]mightily with a loud voice, saying, [a]"Babylon the great is fallen, is fallen, and [b]has become a dwelling place of demons, a prison for every foul spirit, and [c]a cage for every unclean and hated bird! [3]For all the nations [a]have drunk of the wine of the wrath of her fornication, the kings of the earth have committed fornication with her, [b]and the merchants of the earth have become rich through the [1]abundance of her luxury."

[4]And I heard another voice from heaven saying, [a]"Come out of her, my people, lest you share in her sins, and lest you receive of her plagues. [5a]For her sins [1]have reached to heaven, and [b]God has remembered her iniquities. [6a]Render to her just as she rendered [1]to you, and repay her double according to her works; [b]in the cup which she has mixed, [c]mix double for her. [7a]In the measure that she glorified herself and lived [1]luxuriously, in the same measure give her torment and sorrow; for she says in her heart, 'I sit *as* [b]queen, and am no widow, and will not see sorrow.' [8]Therefore her plagues will come [a]in one day—death and mourning and famine. And [b]she will be utterly burned with fire, [c]for strong *is* the Lord God who [1]judges her.

The World Mourns Babylon's Fall

[9a]"The kings of the earth who committed fornication and lived luxuriously with her [b]will weep and lament for her, [c]when they see the smoke of her burning, [10]standing at a distance for fear of her torment, saying, [a]'Alas, alas, that great city Babylon, that mighty city! [b]For in one hour your judgment has come.'

17:14 [b]Rev. 19:20　[c]1 Tim. 6:15　[d]Jer. 50:44　17:15 [a]Is. 8:7　[b]Rev. 13:7　17:16 [a]Jer. 50:41　[b]Rev. 18:17, 19　[c]Ezek. 16:37, 39　[d]Rev. 18:8　[1]NU, M *saw, and the beast*　17:17 [a]2 Thess. 2:11　[b]Rev. 10:7　17:18 [a]Rev. 11:8; 16:19　[b]Rev. 12:4　18:1 [a]Rev. 17:1, 7　[b]Ezek. 43:2　18:2 [a]Is. 13:19; 21:9　[b]Is. 13:21; 34:11, 13–15　[c]Is. 14:23　[1]NU, M omit *mightily*　18:3 [a]Rev. 14:8　[b]Is. 47:15　[1]Lit. *strengths*　18:4 [a]Is. 48:20　18:5 [a]Gen. 18:20　[b]Rev. 16:19　[1]NU, M *have been heaped up*　18:6 [a]Ps. 137:8　[b]Rev. 14:10　[c]Rev. 16:19　[1]NU, M omit *to you*　18:7 [a]Ezek. 28:2–8　[b]Is. 47:7, 8　[1]*sensually*　18:8 [a]Rev. 18:10　[b]Rev. 17:16　[c]Jer. 50:34　[1]NU, M *has judged*　18:9 [a]Ezek. 26:16; 27:35　[b]Jer. 50:46　[c]Rev. 19:3　18:10 [a]Is. 21:9　[b]Rev. 18:17, 19

├─────────────────────┤　LIFE LESSONS　├─────────────────────┤

■ **17:17** — Although the Lord will give the wicked "over to a debased mind, to do those things which are not fitting" (Rom. 1:28), it does not mean He relinquishes all control over them. Ultimately, no one can do anything outside of God's permissive will, and He can even use the alliance of evil rulers to serve His eternal purposes and glorify Himself.

■ **18:2** — The original empire of Babylon was responsible for the destruction of Jerusalem and the temple and the deportation and captivity of her people in 586 B.C. (2 Kin. 25:8, 9; 2 Chr. 36:16–21). It was decadent, wicked, and idolatrous. The name *Babylon* came to represent the evil system of the world that the Enemy uses to oppose God.

Yet there will come a time when Babylon is no more.

■ **18:4** — During the last days, Babylon will be an exceedingly wealthy society, which will also be perverse and demonic. Though tribulation Christians might be tempted to participate in her affluence and wickedness, they are warned to avoid her at all costs, for "she will be utterly burned with fire, for strong is the Lord God who judges her" (Rev. 18:8). Likewise, believers may be tempted to compromise their beliefs for a life that seems to promise immediate pleasure without penalty. However, there are always consequences to sin, and usually they are worse than we can imagine.

¹¹"And ᵃthe merchants of the earth will weep and mourn over her, for no one buys their merchandise anymore: ¹²ᵃmerchandise of gold and silver, precious stones and pearls, fine linen and purple, silk and scarlet, every kind of citron wood, every kind of object of ivory, every kind of object of most precious wood, bronze, iron, and marble; ¹³and cinnamon and incense, fragrant oil and frankincense, wine and oil, fine flour and wheat, cattle and sheep, horses and chariots, and bodies and ᵃsouls of men. ¹⁴The fruit that your soul longed for has gone from you, and all the things which are rich and splendid have ¹gone from you, and you shall find them no more at all. ¹⁵The merchants of these things, who became rich by her, will stand at a distance for fear of her torment, weeping and wailing, ¹⁶and saying, 'Alas, alas, ᵃthat great city ᵇthat was clothed in fine linen, purple, and scarlet, and adorned with gold and precious stones and pearls! ¹⁷ᵃFor in one hour such great riches ¹came to nothing.' ᵇEvery shipmaster, all who travel by ship, sailors, and as many as trade on the sea, stood at a distance ¹⁸ᵃand cried out when they saw the smoke of her burning, saying, ᵇ'What is like this great city?'

¹⁹ᵃ"They threw dust on their heads and cried out, weeping and wailing, and saying, 'Alas, alas, that great city, in which all who had ships on the sea became rich by her wealth! ᵇFor in one hour she ¹is made desolate.'

²⁰ᵃ"Rejoice over her, O heaven, and you ¹holy apostles and prophets, for ᵇGod has avenged you on her!"

Finality of Babylon's Fall

²¹Then a mighty angel took up a stone like a great millstone and threw it into the sea, saying, ᵃ'"Thus with violence the great city Babylon shall be thrown down, and ᵇshall not be found anymore. ²²ᵃThe sound of harpists, musicians, flutists, and trumpeters shall not be heard in you anymore. No craftsman of any craft shall be found in you anymore, and the sound of a millstone shall not be heard in you anymore. ²³ᵃThe light of a lamp shall not shine in you anymore, ᵇand the voice of bridegroom and bride shall not be heard in you anymore. For ᶜyour merchants were the great men of the earth, ᵈfor by your sorcery all the nations were deceived. ²⁴And ᵃin her was found the blood of prophets and saints, and of all who ᵇwere slain on the earth."

Heaven Exults over Babylon

19 After these things ᵃI ¹heard a loud voice of a great multitude in heaven, saying, "Alleluia! ᵇSalvation and glory and honor and power *belong* to ²the Lord our God! ²For ᵃtrue and righteous *are* His judgments, because He has judged the great harlot who corrupted the earth with her fornication; and He ᵇhas avenged on her the blood of His servants *shed* by her." ³Again they said, "Alleluia! ᵃHer smoke rises up forever and ever!" ⁴And ᵃthe twenty-four elders and the four living creatures fell down and worshiped God who sat on the throne, saying, ᵇ"Amen! Alleluia!" ⁵Then a voice came from the throne, saying, ᵃ'"Praise our God, all you His servants

18:11 ᵃ Ezek. 27:27–34 18:12 ᵃ Rev. 17:4 18:13 ᵃ Ezek. 27:13 18:14 ¹ NU, M *been lost to you* 18:16 ᵃ Rev. 17:18 ᵇ Rev. 17:4 18:17 ᵃ Rev. 18:10 ᵇ Is. 23:14 ¹ *have been laid waste* 18:18 ᵃ Ezek. 27:30 ᵇ Rev. 13:4 18:19 ᵃ Josh. 7:6 ᵇ Rev. 18:8 ¹ *have been laid waste* 18:20 ᵃ Jer. 51:48 ᵇ Luke 11:49 ¹ NU, M *saints and apostles* 18:21 ᵃ Jer. 51:63, 64 ᵇ Rev. 12:8; 16:20 18:22 ᵃ Jer. 7:34; 16:9; 25:10 18:23 ᵃ Jer. 25:10 ᵇ Jer. 7:34; 16:9 ᶜ Is. 23:8 ᵈ 2 Kin. 9:22 18:24 ᵃ Rev. 16:6; 17:6 ᵇ Jer. 51:49 19:1 ᵃ Rev. 11:15; 19:6 ᵇ Rev. 4:11 ¹ NU, M add *something like* ²NU, M omit *the Lord* 19:2 ᵃ Rev. 15:3; 16:7 ᵇ Deut. 32:43 19:3 ᵃ Is. 34:10 19:4 ᵃ Rev. 4:4, 6, 10 ᵇ 1 Chr. 16:36 19:5 ᵃ Ps. 134:1

⊢ LIFE LESSONS ⊢

■ **18:24** —Vindication may not come in the manner we expect, but eventually the Lord's judgment will fall on all who persecute His faithful servants (Rom. 12:19; Rev. 19:2).

■ **19:1** —Revelation 19 begins with the glorious praise and worship of the Lord Jesus by the great multitude of heaven. These declarations of His glory usher in His Second Coming.

■ **19:5** —While many differences may separate us here on earth, when we worship before the Lord in heaven, we will approach His throne with unity of heart, mind, and soul. We will exclaim

53

ANSWERS
TO LIFE'S QUESTIONS

CAN THE DEVIL REALLY MAKE ME DO SOMETHING?

| Rev. 18:23 |

The late comedian Flip Wilson may have popularized the catchphrase, "The devil made me do it," but this excuse has always been around. We blame Satan since we know he has something to do with the temptation process.

But in fact, the devil cannot *make* us do anything. The Bible calls Satan a deceiver (Gen. 3:13; 2 Cor. 11:3; Rev. 18:23) and a "liar and the father of it" (John 8:44). Satan's only power over us is through manipulation and deceit.

If the devil could actually *make* us do things, then he wouldn't need to go to all the trouble of deceiving us. When he dangles the right bait in front of us at the right time, our fleshly desires make it seem as though something is relentlessly drawing us toward sin; but this power does not control us. In each case we *choose* to disobey.

Think of it this way. Imagine yourself standing at the edge of a cliff that drops off into a deep, rocky gorge. Now suppose I walked up to you and said, "We have kidnapped a member of your family. If you refuse to jump, your relative will be brutally beaten and then killed." Have I made you jump? If you believed my story and you believed that by jumping you could save your family member, I may have made you *willing* to jump or even *anxious* to jump. But I have not *caused* you to jump. Even if you jumped and you found out on the way to the bottom that I had lied about the whole thing, I still did not *make* you jump. I simply tricked you into jumping. On the other hand, if I walked up behind you and pushed you, then I made you do some-

thing contrary to what you wanted to do, felt like doing, or even thought about doing.

Now think about the last time you felt tempted to sin. Did you suddenly discover that you were sinning or had sinned? Were you in the process before you ever thought about it? Or did it begin with a thought, then a feeling, then maybe a little struggle, then the actual sin?

Just as no one held Eve and forced her to bite the fruit, no one holds you down and forces you to sin. Satan cannot *make* you do anything, but he will do all he can to deceive you into dishonoring God.

Life Principle for further study:

2. OBEY GOD AND LEAVE ALL THE CONSEQUENCES TO HIM.

and those who fear Him, *b*both[1] small and great!"

6*a*And I heard, as it were, the voice of a great multitude, as the sound of many waters and as the sound of mighty thunderings, saying, "Alleluia! For *b*the[1] Lord God Omnipotent reigns! 7Let us be glad and rejoice and give Him glory, for *a*the marriage of the Lamb has come, and His wife has made herself ready." 8And *a*to her it was granted to be arrayed in fine linen, clean and bright, *b*for the fine linen is the righteous acts of the saints.

9Then he said to me, "Write: *a*'Blessed *are* those who are called to the marriage supper of the Lamb!'" And he said to me, *b*"These are the true sayings of God." 10And *a*I fell at his feet to worship him. But he said to me, *b*"See *that you do* not *do that!* I am your *c*fellow servant, and of your brethren *d*who have the testimony of Jesus. Worship God! For the *e*testimony of Jesus is the spirit of prophecy."

Christ on a White Horse

11*a*Now I saw heaven opened, and behold, *b*a white horse. And He who sat on him *was* called *c*Faithful and True, and *d*in righteousness He judges and makes war. 12*a*His eyes *were* like a flame of fire, and on His head *were* many crowns. *b*He [1]had a name written that no one knew except Himself. 13*a*He *was* clothed with a robe dipped in blood, and His name is called *b*The Word of God. 14*a*And the armies in heaven, *b*clothed in [1]fine linen, white and clean, followed Him on white horses. 15Now *a*out of His mouth goes a [1]sharp sword, that with it He should strike the nations. And *b*He Himself will rule them with a rod of iron. *c*He Himself treads the winepress of the fierceness and wrath of Almighty God. 16And *a*He has on *His* robe and on His thigh a name written:

*b*KING OF KINGS AND
LORD OF LORDS.

19:5 *b* Rev. 11:18 [1]NU, M omit *both*   19:6 *a* Ezek. 1:24 *b* Rev. 11:15 [1]NU, M *our*   19:7 *a* [Matt. 22:2; 25:10]   19:8 *a* Ezek. 16:10 *b* Ps. 132:9   19:9 *a* Luke 14:15 *b* Rev. 22:6   19:10 *a* Rev. 22:8 *b* Acts 10:26 *c* [Heb. 1:14] *d* 1 John 5:10 *e* Luke 24:27   19:11 *a* Rev. 15:5 *b* Rev. 6:2; 19:19, 21 *c* Rev. 3:7, 14 *d* Is. 11:4   19:12 *a* Rev. 1:14 *b* Rev. 2:17; 19:16 [1]M adds *names written, and*   19:13 *a* Is. 63:2, 3 *b* [John 1:1, 14]   19:14 *a* Rev. 14:20 *b* Matt. 28:3 [1]NU, M *pure white linen*   19:15 *a* Is. 11:4 *b* Ps. 2:8, 9 *c* Is. 63:3–6 [1]M *sharp two-edged*   19:16 *a* Rev. 2:17; 19:12 *b* Dan. 2:47

├─────────────── ┤ LIFE LESSONS ├ ───────────────

together the awesomeness of His glory and praise Him for His righteousness and all He has done through His mercy and grace.

■ 19:7 — The relationship between Christ the Bridegroom and His bride, the church, is reflected in the Jewish wedding ceremony that occurs in three general phases. First, the marriage contract is approved by both parties, just as our relationship with Christ begins with our agreement with Him at salvation. Second, the groom leaves to prepare a house for his bride-to-be and returns at an unspecified time to take her to their new home. This is fulfilled at the Rapture (Matt. 25:1–13; John 14:2). The final step is the marriage supper — the actual celebration of the wedding — which is described in Revelation 19:7–9 and 21:9–27.

■ 19:9 — If the church is the bride, then who is invited to the wedding feast? These are most likely the Old Testament saints who were justified by their faith (Rom. 4), the tribulation saints, and the angelic host of heaven.

■ 19:10 — Angels have such majesty and power that human beings sometimes feel tempted to worship them — even someone as mature and

godly as John. But angels know their place. God alone deserves our worship!

■ 19:11 — When Jesus returns, He is not coming back as the gentle Lamb. He will appear as the reigning King, our mighty Warrior, and as the righteous Judge of the living and the dead. Jesus returns with His forces to accomplish all the remaining prophecies and covenants of His Word — establishing His kingdom on earth and destroying evil. He is called Faithful and True because not one of His promises will go unfulfilled.

■ 19:13 — Jesus is God (John 1:1, 2; 10:30). He is also the Word — the Godhead's spoken, incarnate expression of Himself (John 1:18; Heb. 1:2, 3). When the Lord announced that He would save us (Matt. 1:21, 23), His "Word became flesh and dwelt among us" (John 1:14).

■ 19:16 — Ultimately, the war on the plain of Megiddo (Armageddon) is the culmination of the battles God has fought throughout the ages in every heart and against everyone who has served their own prideful will — replacing Him on the throne of their lives with something or someone else (Ex. 20:2–5; Josh. 24:14, 15; 1 Kin. 18:21; Ps.

The Beast and His Armies Defeated

[17]Then I saw an angel standing in the sun; and he cried with a loud voice, saying to all the birds that fly in the midst of heaven, [a]"Come and gather together for the [1]supper of the great God, [18a]that you may eat the flesh of kings, the flesh of captains, the flesh of mighty men, the flesh of horses and of those who sit on them, and the flesh of all *people,* [1]free and slave, both small and great."

[19a]And I saw the beast, the kings of the earth, and their armies, gathered together to make war against Him who sat on the horse and against His army. [20a]Then the beast was captured, and with him the false prophet who worked signs in his presence, by which he deceived those who received the mark of the beast and [b]those who worshiped his image. [c]These two were cast alive into the lake of fire [d]burning with brimstone. [21]And the rest [a]were killed with the sword which proceeded from the mouth of Him who sat on the horse. [b]And all the birds [c]were filled with their flesh.

Satan Bound 1,000 Years

20 Then I saw an angel coming down from heaven, [a]having the key to the bottomless pit and a great chain in his hand. [2]He laid hold of [a]the dragon, that serpent of old, who is *the* Devil and Satan, and bound him for a thousand years; [3]and he cast him into the bottomless pit, and shut him up, and [a]set a seal on him, [b]so that he should deceive the nations no more till the thousand years were finished. But after these things he must be released for a little while.

The Saints Reign with Christ 1,000 Years

[4]And I saw [a]thrones, and they sat on them, and [b]judgment was committed to them. Then *I saw* [c]the souls of those who had been beheaded for their witness to Jesus and for the word of God, [d]who had not worshiped the beast [e]or his image, and had not received *his* mark on their foreheads or on their hands. And they [f]lived and [g]reigned with Christ for [1]a thousand years. [5]But the rest of the dead did not live again until the thousand years were finished. This *is* the first resurrection. [6]Blessed and holy *is* he who has part in the first resurrection. Over such [a]the second death has no power, but they shall be [b]priests of God and of Christ, [c]and shall reign with Him a thousand years.

19:17 [a] Ezek. 39:17 [1] NU, M great supper of God   19:18 [a] Ezek. 39:18–20 [1] NU, M both free   19:19 [a] Rev. 16:13–16   19:20 [a] Rev. 16:13 [b] Rev. 13:8, 12, 13 [c] Dan. 7:11 [d] Rev. 14:10   19:21 [a] Rev. 19:15 [b] Rev. 19:17, 18 [c] Rev. 17:16   20:1 [a] Rev. 1:18; 9:1   20:2 [a] 2 Pet. 2:4   20:3 [a] Dan. 6:17 [b] Rev. 12:9; 20:8, 10   20:4 [a] Dan. 7:9 [b] [1 Cor. 6:2, 3] [c] Rev. 6:9 [d] Rev. 13:12 [e] Rev. 13:15 [f] John 14:19 [g] Rom. 8:17 [1] M the   20:6 [a] [Rev. 2:11; 20:14] [b] Is. 61:6 [c] Rev. 20:4

⊢ LIFE LESSONS ⊢

14:1, 2; Is. 14:13, 14; Matt. 6:24; Rom. 1:21). The Lord Jesus veiled His royal majesty during His years of earthly ministry (Phil. 2:5–11), but He will reveal His glory when He returns, so there will be absolutely no doubt that He is the absolute ruler of all that exists (Ps. 103:19).

■ **19:20** — After His complete victory, the Lord sends the Antichrist and the false prophet to eternal condemnation in the lake of fire, which is hell. Some imagine that those in hell are eventually annihilated, but that is not true. Scripture is clear: "They will be tormented day and night forever and ever" (Rev. 20:10).

■ **20:2** — We blame much of our troubles on the Enemy and the world's system, but if all that were taken away, how would we respond to the Lord? During Christ's millennial reign, we will find out.

An angel binds Satan and imprisons him for one thousand years so he will not be able to deceive people. And God gives humanity one last test to show us that the greatest adversary we have is really within ourselves.

■ **20:3** — Why must Satan be released after his long imprisonment? Why doesn't God judge him immediately? Through the Enemy's rebellion, the hearts of those who only pretend to love the Lord are revealed (Rev. 20:7–9). And then the devil meets his final judgment.

■ **20:5** — This first resurrection is of tribulation saints who will rule with Christ during His millennial reign. The rest of the dead — who will be resurrected at the end of the thousand years — are all unbelievers from the beginning of time.

Satanic Rebellion Crushed

7Now when the thousand years have expired, Satan will be released from his prison **8**and will go out *a*to deceive the nations which are in the four corners of the earth, *b*Gog and Magog, *c*to gather them together to battle, whose number *is* as the sand of the sea. **9***a*They went up on the breadth of the earth and surrounded the camp of the saints and the beloved city. And fire came down from God out of heaven and devoured them. **10**The devil, who deceived them, was cast into the lake of fire and brimstone *a*where*1* the beast and the false prophet *are.* And they *b*will be tormented day and night forever and ever.

The Great White Throne Judgment

11Then I saw a great white throne and Him who sat on it, from whose face *a*the earth and the heaven fled away. *b*And there was found no place for them. **12**And I saw the dead, *a*small and great, standing before *1*God, *b*and books were opened.

And another *c*book was opened, which is *the Book* of Life. And the dead were judged *d*according to their works, by the things which were written in the books. **13**The sea gave up the dead who were in it, *a*and Death and Hades delivered up the dead who were in them. *b*And they were judged, each one according to his works. **14**Then *a*Death and Hades were cast into the lake of fire. *b*This is the second *1*death. **15**And anyone not found written in the Book of Life *a*was cast into the lake of fire.

All Things Made New

21 Now *a*I saw a new heaven and a new earth, *b*for the first heaven and the first earth had passed away. Also there was no more sea. **2**Then I, *1*John, saw *a*the holy city, New Jerusalem, coming down out of heaven from God, prepared *b*as a bride adorned for her husband. **3**And I heard a loud voice from heaven saying, "Behold, *a*the tabernacle of God *is* with men, and He will dwell with them, and they shall be His people. God Himself will be with them

---

20:8 *a* Rev. 12:9; 20:3, 10　*b* Ezek. 38:2; 39:1, 6　*c* Rev. 16:14　20:9 *a* Ezek. 38:9, 16　20:10 *a* Rev. 19:20; 20:14, 15　*b* Rev. 14:10　*1* NU, M *where also*　20:11 *a* 2 Pet. 3:7　*b* Dan. 2:35　20:12 *a* Rev. 19:5　*b* Dan. 7:10　*c* Ps. 69:28　*d* Matt. 16:27　*1* NU, M *the throne*　20:13 *a* Rev. 1:18; 6:8; 21:4　*b* Rev. 2:23; 20:12　20:14 *a* 1 Cor. 15:26　*b* Rev. 21:8　*1* NU, M *death, the lake of fire.*　20:15 *a* Rev. 19:20　21:1 *a* [2 Pet. 3:13]　*b* Rev. 20:11　21:2 *a* Is. 52:1　*b* 2 Cor. 11:2　*1* NU, M omit *John*　21:3 *a* Lev. 26:11

┤ LIFE LESSONS ├

■ **20:10** — Jesus said, "I will build My church, and the gates of Hades shall not prevail against it" (Matt. 16:18). Here we see Christ's final victory over the Enemy. Satan is a defeated foe. Although we still fight against him and he will continue trying to undermine the truth of the gospel, we know for certain that he will ultimately lose the battle.

■ **20:11** — Some believe that at the Great White Throne Judgment, they will be able to air their complaints and excuses to God. However, that is not the case. Thankfully, we who believe in Jesus Christ as our Savior have our names written in the Lamb's Book of Life and have absolutely no reason to fear. We are assured that we will enjoy heaven with Him forever.

■ **20:12** — At the Great White Throne, everyone is judged according to whether or not they've accepted Christ as their Savior and their name is written in the Lamb's Book of Life. Those who have been redeemed are welcomed into heaven. Those who refuse to believe in Christ must bear the penalty of their sin and are cast into the lake

of fire (John 3:18; Rom. 6:23). There is no board of appeals in heaven. Once we appear before Christ, our character and eternal destination are fixed.

■ **20:15** — All judgment has been committed to Jesus Christ (John 5:22) because He knows us perfectly and is just, holy, honest, and trustworthy. Those who place their faith in Him will never be disappointed. Rather, their names are permanently and irrevocably written in the Lamb's Book of Life (Rev. 21:27). Those who depend on their own efforts to reach heaven will instead find themselves in the lake of fire — eternally separated from God.

■ **21:1** — Heaven and earth are not annihilated; they are completely and perfectly cleansed — renewed like they were in the garden of Eden before the fall of Adam and Eve (Rev. 21:5).

■ **21:3** — The best part of the New Jerusalem will not be the streets of gold, the pearly gates, or even the happy reunions we will enjoy with believing loved ones. The best thing about heaven is the loving presence of God Himself.

and be their God. [4a]And God will wipe away every tear from their eyes; [b]there shall be no more death, [c]nor sorrow, nor crying. There shall be no more pain, for the former things have passed away."

[5]Then [a]He who sat on the throne said, [b]"Behold, I make all things new." And He said [1]to me, "Write, for [c]these words are true and faithful."

[6]And He said to me, [a]"It[1] is done! [b]I am the Alpha and the Omega, the Beginning and the End. [c]I will give of the fountain of the water of life freely to him who thirsts. [7]He who overcomes [1]shall inherit all things, and [a]I will be his God and he shall be My son. [8a]But the cowardly, [1]unbelieving, abominable, murderers, sexually immoral, sorcerers, idolaters, and all liars shall have their part in [b]the lake which burns with fire and brimstone, which is the second death."

The New Jerusalem

[9]Then one of [a]the seven angels who had the seven bowls filled with the seven last plagues came [1]to me and talked with me, saying, "Come, I will show you [b]the [2]bride, the Lamb's wife." [10]And he carried me away [a]in the Spirit to a great and high mountain, and showed me [b]the [1]great city, the [2]holy Jerusalem, descending out of heaven from God, [11a]having the glory of God. Her light *was* like a most precious stone, like a jasper stone, clear as crystal. [12]Also she had a great and high wall with [a]twelve gates, and twelve angels at the gates, and names written on them, which are *the names* of the twelve tribes of the children of Israel: [13a]three gates on the east, three gates on the north, three gates on the south, and three gates on the west. [14]Now the wall of the city had twelve foundations, and [a]on them were the [1]names of the twelve apostles of the Lamb. [15]And he who talked with me [a]had a gold reed to measure the city, its gates, and its wall. [16]The city is laid out as a square; its length is as great as its breadth. And he measured the city with the reed: twelve thousand [1]furlongs. Its length, breadth, and height are equal. [17]Then he measured its wall: one hundred *and* forty-four cubits, *according* to the measure of a man, that is, of an angel. [18]The construction of its wall was *of* jasper; and the city *was* pure gold, like clear glass. [19a]The foundations of the wall of the city *were* adorned with all kinds of precious stones: the first foundation *was* jasper, the second sapphire, the third chalcedony, the fourth emerald, [20]the fifth sardonyx, the sixth sardius, the seventh chrysolite, the eighth beryl, the ninth topaz, the tenth chrysoprase, the eleventh jacinth, and the twelfth amethyst. [21]The twelve gates *were* twelve [a]pearls: each individual gate was of one pearl. [b]And the street of the city *was* pure gold, like transparent glass.

The Glory of the New Jerusalem

[22a]But I saw no temple in it, for the Lord God Almighty and the Lamb are its

21:4 [a]Is. 25:8 [b1]Cor. 15:26 [c]Is. 35:10; 51:11; 65:19 21:5 [a]Rev. 4:2, 9; 20:11 [b]Is. 43:19 [c]Rev. 19:9; 22:6 [1]NU, M omit *to me* 21:6 [a]Rev. 10:6; 16:17 [b]Rev. 1:8; 22:13 [c]John 4:10 [1]M omits *It is done* 21:7 [a]Zech. 8:8 [1]M *I shall give him these things* 21:8 [a1]Cor. 6:9 [b]Rev. 20:14 [1]M adds *and sinners,* 21:9 [a]Rev. 15:1 [b]Rev. 19:7; 21:2 [1]NU, M omit *to me* [2]M *woman, the Lamb's bride* 21:10 [a]Rev. 1:10 [b]Ezek. 48 [1]NU, M omit *great* [2]NU, M *holy city, Jerusalem* 21:11 [a]Rev. 15:8; 21:23; 22:5 21:12 [a]Ezek. 48:31–34 21:13 [a]Ezek. 48:31–34 21:14 [a]Eph. 2:20 [1]NU, M *twelve names* 21:15 [a]Ezek. 40:3 21:16 [1]Lit. *stadia,* about 1,380 miles in all 21:19 [a]Is. 54:11 21:21 [a]Matt. 13:45, 46 [b]Rev. 22:2 21:22 [a]John 4:21, 23

─────────────┤ LIFE LESSONS ├─────────────

■ 21:4 — Our eternal home is like nothing we've ever experienced before because it is a place that is free from sin, death, fear, guilt, and sorrow. Never again will we experience the consequences of our fallen nature — separation from our loved ones, loss, worry, sickness, crime, pain, or injustice. Rather, we will be absolutely free to become all God created us to be — to His praise and glory.

And best of all, we will enjoy full, wonderful fellowship with our Lord and Savior forever.

■ 21:7 — As the adopted children of God (Eph. 1:5), we are "heirs of God and joint heirs with Christ"; and we overcome when we "suffer with Him, that we may also be glorified together" (Rom. 8:17).

temple. ^{23a}The city had no need of the sun or of the moon to shine ¹in it, for the ²glory of God illuminated it. The Lamb *is* its light. ^{24a}And the nations ¹of those who are saved shall walk in its light, and the kings of the earth bring their glory and honor ²into it. ^{25a}Its gates shall not be shut at all by day ^b(there shall be no night there). ^{26a}And they shall bring the glory and the honor of the nations into ¹it. ²⁷But ^athere shall by no means enter it anything ¹that defiles, or causes an abomination or a lie, but only those who are written in the Lamb's ^bBook of Life.

The River of Life

22 And he showed me ^aa ¹pure river of water of life, clear as crystal, proceeding from the throne of God and of the Lamb. ^{2a}In the middle of its street, and on either side of the river, *was* ^bthe tree of life, which bore twelve fruits, each *tree* yielding its fruit every month. The leaves of the tree *were* ^cfor the healing of the nations. ³And ^athere shall be no more curse, ^bbut the throne of God and of the Lamb shall be in it, and His ^cservants shall serve Him. ^{4a}They shall see His face, and ^bHis name *shall be* on their foreheads. ^{5a}There shall be no night there: They need no lamp nor ^blight of the sun, for ^cthe Lord God gives them light. ^dAnd they shall reign forever and ever.

The Time Is Near

⁶Then he said to me, ^a"These words *are* faithful and true." And the Lord God of the ¹holy prophets ^bsent His angel to show His servants the things which must ^cshortly take place.

^{7a}"Behold, I am coming quickly! ^bBlessed *is* he who keeps the words of the prophecy of this book."

⁸Now I, John, ¹saw and heard these things. And when I heard and saw, ^aI fell down to worship before the feet of the angel who showed me these things.

⁹Then he said to me, ^a"See *that you do* not *do that.* ¹For I am your fellow servant, and of your brethren the prophets, and of those who keep the words of this book. Worship God." ^{10a}And he said to me, "Do not seal the words of the prophecy of this book, ^bfor the time is at hand. ¹¹He who is unjust, let him be unjust still; he who is filthy, let him be filthy still; he who is righteous, let him ¹be righteous still; he who is holy, let him be holy still."

Jesus Testifies to the Churches

¹²"And behold, I am coming quickly, and ^aMy reward *is* with Me, ^bto give to every one according to his work. ^{13a}I am

21:23 ^a Is. 24:23; 60:19, 20 ¹ NU, M omit *in it* ² M *very glory* 21:24 ^a Is. 60:3, 5; 66:12 ¹ NU, M omit *of those who are saved* ² M *of the nations to Him* 21:25 ^a Is. 60:11 ^b Is. 60:20 21:26 ^a Rev. 21:24 ¹ M adds *that they may enter in.* 21:27 ^a Joel 3:17 ^b Phil. 4:3 ¹ NU, M *profane, nor one who causes* 22:1 ^a Ezek. 47:1 ¹ NU, M omit *pure* 22:2 ^a Ezek. 47:12 ^b Gen. 2:9 ^c Rev. 21:24 22:3 ^a Zech. 14:11 ^b Ezek. 48:35 ^c Rev. 7:15 22:4 ^a [Matt. 5:8] ^b Rev. 14:1 22:5 ^a Rev. 21:23 ^b Rev. 7:15 ^c Ps. 36:9 ^d Dan. 7:18, 27 22:6 ^a Rev. 19:9 ^b Rev. 1:1 ^c Heb. 10:37 ¹ NU, M *spirits of the prophets* 22:7 ^a [Rev. 3:11] ^b Rev. 1:3 22:8 ^a Rev. 19:10 ¹ NU, M *am the one who heard and saw* 22:9 ^a Rev. 19:10 ¹ NU, M omit *For* 22:10 ^a Dan. 8:26 ^b Rev. 1:3 22:11 ¹ NU, M *do right* 22:12 ^a Is. 40:10; 62:11 ^b Rev. 20:12 22:13 ^a Is. 41:4

LIFE LESSONS

■ **21:23**—Genesis 1:3 tells us there was light in this world long before the sun, moon, and stars existed (Gen. 1:16). Likewise, 1 John 1:5 tells us, "God is light and in Him is no darkness at all." Believers will again enjoy the Lord's pure, uninterrupted light in the Holy City, the New Jerusalem, because He will be with us always, and we will never be separated from Him again.

■ **22:3**—What will believers do in heaven? Scripture indicates that we will serve the Lord. But what does this mean? God has given each of us gifts and talents to use, and we will most likely employ them

in some way that will be exceedingly joyful for us. One thing is certain: whatever we do is going to be far better than all we can imagine, to the praise and glory of His name (1 Cor. 2:9; Eph. 3:20).

■ **22:12**—John reminds us that Jesus may return at any moment and repeats that those who hear the words of Revelation and who commit themselves to Spirit-empowered, godly obedience will be greatly blessed (Rev. 1:3). Therefore, an eager anticipation of Christ's return should keep us living productively. We should be motivated and joyful, knowing that Jesus has prepared great

HOW GOD JUDGES AND REWARDS OUR WORK

• Rev. 22:12 •

Though we consider the apostle Paul the greatest missionary in history, he received more lashes and stones than honorary banquets, and he spent more time in jail than in mansions. How did he continue under such duress? He looked ahead to God's reward: "Finally, there is laid up for me the crown of righteousness, which the Lord, the righteous Judge, will give to me on that Day" (2 Tim. 4:8).

Why would Moses leave the luxury of Pharaoh's palace for the harshness of the desert? Because he considered the "reproach of Christ greater riches than the treasures in Egypt; for he looked to the reward" (Heb. 11:26). Serving God yielded Moses a vast storehouse of heavenly reward, though it meant a lifetime of struggle.

Every act, word, and thought will be credited by Christ: "Each one will receive his own reward according to his own labor" (1 Cor. 3:8). If we seek to glorify God with a diligent and humble spirit, our laurels will multiply. If we seek merely to please others and reap their praise, then our rewards will shrink.

Rewards are not limited to the hereafter. Whenever we follow the principles of Scripture, we enjoy the blessings of obedience: "He who fears the commandment will be rewarded" (Prov. 13:13).

When Peter reminded Jesus that he had left everything behind to follow the Messiah, Christ responded, "There is no one who has left house or parents or brothers or wife or children, for the sake of the kingdom of God, who shall not receive many times more in this present time, and in the age to come eternal life" (Luke 18:29, 30).

When one knows and serves God, every product of his or her life will be rewarded, either in this life or in heaven.

God watches over all our ways, and He has promised to perfectly reward us. All those who "serve the Lord Christ" (Col. 3:24) will be rewarded on the day of judgment of believers. The Christian who seeks to please God lays up treasures that can never be devalued or depleted.

Life Principles for further study:

21. OBEDIENCE ALWAYS BRINGS BLESSING.

6. YOU REAP WHAT YOU SOW, MORE THAN YOU SOW, AND LATER THAN YOU SOW.

GOD WATCHES OVER ALL OUR WAYS.

the Alpha and the Omega, *the* [1]Beginning and *the* End, the First and the Last."

[14a]Blessed *are* those who [1]do His commandments, that they may have the right [b]to the tree of life, [c]and may enter through the gates into the city. [15l]But [a]outside *are* [b]dogs and sorcerers and sexually immoral and murderers and idolaters, and whoever loves and practices a lie.

[16a]"I, Jesus, have sent My angel to testify to you these things in the churches. [b]I am the Root and the Offspring of David, [c]the Bright and Morning Star."

[17]And the Spirit and [a]the bride say, "Come!" And let him who hears say, "Come!" [b]And let him who thirsts come. Whoever desires, let him take the water of life freely.

A Warning

[18l]For I testify to everyone who hears the words of the prophecy of this book: [a]If anyone adds to these things, [2]God will add to him the plagues that are written in this book; [19]and if anyone takes away from the words of the book of this prophecy, [a]God[1] shall take away his part from the [2]Book of Life, from the holy city, and *from* the things which are written in this book.

I Am Coming Quickly

[20]He who testifies to these things says, "Surely I am coming quickly."

Amen. Even so, come, Lord Jesus!

[21]The grace of our Lord Jesus Christ *be* [1]with you all. Amen.

22:13 [1]NU, M *First and the Last, the Beginning and the End.*   22:14 [a]Dan. 12:12 [1]NU *wash their robes,* [b][Prov. 11:30] [c]Rev. 21:27   22:15 [a]1 Cor. 6:9 [b]Phil. 3:2 [1]NU, M omit *But*   22:16 [a]Rev. 1:1 [b]Rev. 5:5 [c]Num. 24:17   22:17 [a][Rev. 21:2, 9] [b]Is. 55:1   22:18 [a]Deut. 4:2; 12:32 [1]NU, M omit *For* [2]M *may God add*   22:19 [a]Ex. 32:33 [1]M *may God take away*   [2]NU, M *tree of life*   22:21 [1]NU *with all;* M *with all the saints*

───────────────┤ LIFE LESSONS ├───────────────

rewards and a wonderful home for us in heaven. One day soon we will see Him face-to-face.

■ **22:14** — All the way through the Bible, from Genesis to Revelation, we learn that obedience to God's commands brings great blessing. We have washed our robes in the blood of the Lamb, and because we have submitted ourselves to the Lord in this, we are invited to eat of the Tree of Life—the very tree Adam and Eve were prevented from partaking of after they sinned (Gen. 3:22–24).

■ **22:17** — Jesus said, "Whoever drinks of the water that I shall give him will never thirst. But the water that I shall give him will become in him a fountain of water springing up into everlasting life" (John 4:14). He is always inviting people to come and partake of the great gift of eternal life

He has given. And as the bride of Christ—the church—we should as well.

■ **22:20** — When will Jesus return? No one can say. Yet Christ's return should not be merely a far-off hope for you. Rather, it should be a daily reminder that God is *always* active in your life. He leaves you on earth after you are saved to grow spiritually in oneness with Him and to lead others to a saving knowledge of Jesus Christ. Is that what you've been busy doing? Have you been seeking and serving Him, remembering the awesome reward that awaits you in heaven? When you meet Jesus, you will know and understand that the greatest riches of this fallen world cannot be compared to the glory of being in His presence. Everything pales in comparison to this.

• LIFE PRINCIPLE 30 •

• • •

AN EAGER ANTICIPATION OF THE LORD'S RETURN KEEPS US LIVING PRODUCTIVELY.

| Rev. 22:12 |

• • •

Throughout Scripture we find three admonitions given to us about the Lord's return:

Watch faithfully.

Work diligently.

Wait peacefully.

1. We are to watch.

The Lord said repeatedly that we are to watch for His coming because we do not know the day or hour of His return (Matt. 24:42; 25:13). In Luke 21:36, Jesus gave this specific instruction: "Watch therefore, and pray always that you may be counted worthy to escape all these things that will come to pass, and to stand before the Son of Man."

We are to do more than pray as we watch. We are to stand fast in the faith with bravery and strength (1 Cor. 16:13). We are to watch soberly, arming ourselves with faith, love, and salvation (1 Thess. 5:8). As we watch, we are to remain especially aware of false prophets. We are to discern the spirits and to reject soundly all who do not confess that Jesus Christ is God in the flesh (2 Pet. 2:1; 1 John 4:1–2).

Jesus spoke to John in a vision and gave this great promise to those who remain watchful: "Behold, I am coming as a thief. Blessed is he who watches" (Rev. 16:15).

2. We are to work.

Why does Jesus leave us here on earth after He saves us? Why aren't we born again, then immediately taken into the Lord's presence? Because we still have work to do!

First, God calls us to win souls. We are to be the Lord's witnesses—telling of the love of God and the atoning death of Jesus Christ. We are to testify about what He has done in our own lives, both with our words and by our examples. So long as there remains a soul on earth who hasn't heard the gospel of our Lord Jesus Christ, we have work to do!

Second, we are to grow spiritually, developing an ever-increasing intimacy with the Lord. None of us fully lives up to our spiritual potential. We *all* have room to grow. In those areas where we discover we are unlike Christ, we must work with the Spirit to become conformed to His likeness. Our minds must be renewed (Rom. 12:2). Our inner hurts and emotions must be healed. We must grow in spiritual discernment and in the wisdom of God. Our faith must be strengthened and used so that our prayers and our actions more effectively build up the Lord's kingdom.

3. We are to wait.

Waiting isn't easy. Impatience often leads to frustration. Waiting can also cause a buildup of fear. The longer something anticipated doesn't happen, the greater our concern grows with what will happen, which can degenerate into worry

We do not know the day or hour of His return.

over what might happen. And fear is only a step away.

The angels spoke peace to the earth at Jesus' first coming (Luke 2:14). More than four hundred times in Scripture, the Lord says that we are not to fear, but to enjoy peace. The prophet Isaiah referred to Jesus as the Prince of Peace (Is. 9:6). Throughout His ministry, the Lord Jesus spoke peace. To the woman with an issue of blood He said, "Go in peace" (Mark 5:34); to a stormy sea He said, "Peace, be still" (Mark 4:39); and to His disciples He said, "My peace I give to you" (John 14:27). The Lord calls us to peace as we await His return.

Apart from Jesus, there is no peace—not within a human heart and not among human beings or nations. With Jesus, we can experience peace that surpasses our rational capacity and settles deep within (Phil. 4:7). We are to seek and find this peace as we await the Lord's return.

When the Lord comes, will He find you among those who love Him and call Him Savior and Lord?

When the Lord comes, will He find you doing what He has commanded you to do?

When the Lord comes, will He find you eager to see Him?

When the Lord comes, will He find you ready for His appearing?

When the Lord calls with a shout from heaven, will you instantly rise to be with Him?

When the Lord appears in the clouds, will your heart rejoice with exceedingly great joy?

You have it within your grasp to positively answer these questions. How will you choose to respond to the Lord's challenges upon your life?

The fact is, He is coming again!

See the Life Principles Index in the full study Bible for further study.

When the Lord comes, will He find you eager to see Him?